A Thousand Sundays

Also by Jerry Bowles

FOREVER HOLD YOUR BANNER HIGH

A Thousand Sundays

The Story of The Ed Sullivan Show

Jerry Bowles

G. P. PUTNAM'S SONS
NEW YORK

"Hymn for a Sunday Evening" (Ed Sullivan) from *Bye Bye Birdie* by
Lee Adams & Charles Strouse, © 1960, 1963 Lee Adams & Charles
Strouse. All rights throughout the world controlled by Edwin H.
Morris & Company, A Division of MPL Communications, Inc.
International Copyright Secured. All rights reserved. Used by
Permission.

Library of Congress Cataloging in Publication Data

Bowles, Jerry G
    A thousand Sundays.

    1. Ed Sullivan show (Television program)
2.   Sullivan, Ed. 1902–1974   3.   Television personalities
—United States—Biography.   I.   Ed Sullivan show
(Television program)   II.   Title.
PN1992.77.E35B6   791.45'72   79-28213
ISBN 0-399-12493-4

For Suzanne, as always

Acknowledgments

No book of this sort is possible without the cooperation of dozens of people. I am especially indebted to the Sullivan family—Bob and Betty Precht, Helen Culyer, and—indeed—Carmine Santullo—for allowing me to ask many questions and for answering them all as candidly as they did. I also want to thank the many people who worked with and for Sullivan for sharing their memories with me.

My wife Suzanne helped enormously with the research and with love and support throughout the project.

Also, my thanks to Thekla Christopher for assistance in preparation of the manuscript, to the Museum of Broadcasting, and to the Lincoln Center Branch of the New York Public Library, especially Don Madison.

Finally, a thank you to my editors John Stillman and Judy Wederholt.

Contents

Part III The Ed Sullivan Show:1955–1971

Prologue

Television, it is sometimes said, killed vaudeville. Perhaps this is so. One pictures a sad-eyed old man, alone with his tabby in some cold water walk-up, passing his evenings poring over old Roxy programs, recalling his seat on the aisle at Loew's State and the golden days of the comics and jugglers and the doll-faced lady singers with the ostrich feathers in their hats.

How incredibly sad. One wishes that the poor fellow had only owned a television set. Because if television was, indeed, the murderous hand at the throat of vaudeville, it was not a fast kill. For twenty-three glorious years, from June 20, 1948 to June 6, 1971, vaudeville lived on—cleverly disguised as a TV show, but vaudeville nonetheless—every Sunday night at eight on the CBS network, its curator a glum Irishman named Ed Sullivan.

What an unlikely star this Sullivan was, awkward and uncomfortable in the limelight, his voice a high-pitched New Yorkese that wavered frequently to the tolerable limits of pitch. A first-time viewer might easily surmise that the regular host had failed to show this particular night and that the producers, in a moment of absolute desperation, had cornered the night security guard, pressed him into a Dunhill suit, and shoved him out on a stage to face the waiting television eye.

Surely few among the scant thousands who saw that first broadcast in June 1948 would have guessed that this man was already a thirty-year veteran of vaudeville stages, that show business was his chosen profession, and that he, in fact, enjoyed, even relished, the idea of appearing before audiences.

There is something charming about this Sullivan's lack of stage guile. He is obviously a theater buff—a performer at heart if not in presence. See the curious pride with which he returns to the camera after the guys have finished twirling the plates atop the sticks. "Let's really hear it," he says, and his voice conveys a genuine awe. How lucky we are, you and I, it says, to be in the presence of people who are able to display so damned much talent in public.

It is precisely this lack of guile, coupled with extraordinary talent as a producer, that explains Sullivan's longevity as a television star. He knew what the public wanted to see and he brought it to them. He was so grateful simply to have a seat right up on stage that he never overstayed his welcome.

From his newspapering career, he brought to the show a love of the "timely." Let some over-eager football rookie jump off the bench to tackle a rival halfback on his way to a sure touchtown and you could bet that next Sunday that maladroit rookie would be on the Sullivan stage, sandwiched between the dancing bears and a comic lamenting his mother-in-law. Some young lady from Manly, Iowa, has a steer named Shorty who has just won a big prize at an International Livestock Exposition in Chicago. She'll be there and so, indeed, will Shorty. Sullivan will introduce the steer with the same pride and awe with which he might bring on Maria Callas fresh from a triumph at La Scala.

And on it goes, year after dizzy year. The parade of singers, dancers, jugglers, tumblers, trained animals of all descriptions, seems endless. The Sullivan show grows in popularity and becomes not merely a TV entertainment but an American institution. For performers, an appearance with Sullivan becomes essential to success in the business.

Sullivan is often credited with being a great discoverer of talent. This is not true. The show was never a springboard to fame for unknowns. Bob Hope, Humphrey Bogart, Alfred Lunt and Lynn Fontanne, even the Beatles, were hardly out of work when they arrived, full-blown, on the Sullivan stage. For the great wash of performers, though, the Sullivan show was a confirmation of their stature, a signal to the world that they had arrived. The kid's been on the Sullivan show? Fine, he's a member of the club.

For most, that fame was fleeting. The list of performers who went from the Sullivan show to oblivion is far longer than a list of those who remained in the public eye.

But that, of course, was not Sullivan's fault. He gave us what we wanted when we wanted to see it. Our fickleness concerned him only to the degree that he personally might fall into our disfavor. He wanted only to please.

Before the coming of public television, Sullivan was our primary introduction to the high arts. He brought us the likes of Rudolph Nureyev, Margot Fonteyn, and the great Russian Moiseyev Ballet. Roberta Peters and Maria Callas were there— right after the great dog act from Miami, but indisputably there. Excerpts from Broadway shows, Charles Laughton reading from The Bible—they were there, too. He spent more money than he had to bring pianist Eugene List from Potsdam for the first telecast. It is said that Sullivan did more to introduce the American heartland to culture than any other personality in the history of television. If that is so, one can thank the catholic nature of his show. Something for everybody was his credo. If you didn't like the performer who was on now you could wait five minutes and there would be a new one.

He was also, in a curious way, one of the fathers of rock music. Elvis had been on TV several times before he arrived at the Sullivan show but none of his appearances had anything like the impact of that performance. The Beatles never really took off in the United States until they received the Sullivan confirmation of stature.

The story of the Sullivan show is more than simply a biography of Ed Sullivan, of course. Sullivan was the show's visible symbol. He demanded, and got, credit for almost everything that happened on it.

But the reality is more complex than that. There were hundreds of people involved in the making of the television show that became an American institution. Some of their stories are in this book.

Part I

Toast of the Town: 1948–1955

The King of Sunday Night

The story of Ed Sullivan's beginning in television is so improbable that it might begin "once upon a time. . . ." Yet almost everyone connected with the event swears it is true.

This much is certain: in 1947, Sullivan was forty-six years old and, by his own standards, a failure. He had failed in radio, in motion pictures, and he had never even come close to achieving as a newspaper columnist the kind of following enjoyed by his arch rival, Walter Winchell. He was fairly well known, of course. His column ran in the New York *Daily News* and about thirty other papers around the country; he could still headline shows at Loew's State and the Roxy; and he could muster a decent income. He was an intelligent man, though, and he realized that his lifeboat was welded to the sides of two sinking ships; vaudeville, which he believed would never be able to survive a serious challenge from the little tube in the living room, and the popularity of gossip columns, a medium already on the wane.

He began having a recurring dream about walking into the "morgue"—the newspaper library—at the *Daily News* and asking a gray-haired old man to find some clippings only to realize that the gray-haired old man was himself.

Fortunately for Sullivan, it was not to be. Fate, in the person of a bookish, rotund and balding intellectual named Worthington Miner, was to alter the course of Sullivan's life. Miner—Tony, to his friends—had been involved in television since its earliest pre-World War II days. In the spring of 1948 Miner became manager of Program Development for CBS. His specific charge: create a major musical variety show and a major dramatic show. The dramatic show turned out to be the highly acclaimed *Studio One*. The variety show was, of course, *Toast of the Town*. But that's getting ahead of the story.

CBS-TV in those days consisted of a series of cubicles at 485 Madison Avenue, some improvised studio space in the lofty reaches of Grand Central Station, and leased space in vacant legitimate and movie theaters around New York.

The opening of the CBS eye had been delayed somewhat by the desire of its president, William Paley, to perfect a color system or, more specifically, to beat RCA-NBC in the peacock stakes. CBS ultimately lost that race but that's another story, covered brilliantly in Erik Barnouw's *Tube of Plenty*.

By early 1948, however, it became clear that the public demand for programming was running well ahead of development of the CBS color system. The telecast of the 1947 World Series had been a tremendous success and NBC was getting ready to launch *Texaco Star Theatre* starring Milton Berle, which was to eliminate Tuesday night business for the restaurants and movie theaters in the cities where it was seen.

Miner despaired of finding another comic as crafty, or as instinctively at home in the new medium, as Berle. He realized that whoever he came up with, that person would inevitably be compared to Berle and the results could be disastrous. Most comedians, he realized, did "acts" and once that had been seen

22

by the TV audience, there would be a serious problem about what to do the next week. It was then that he hit upon the concept of having the host be a "discoverer" of talent, not necessarily a talent himself.

By chance CBS happened to be doing its first remote broadcast from Madison Square Garden. It was the Harvest Moon Ball with Ed Sullivan as emcee. All his life Sullivan swore that he didn't know he was on television that night. Considering his lack of aptitude for things mechanical, the story is plausible.

"Somebody told me to work to the cameras," he later said, "but I thought they were newsreel cameras—not live television."

Tony Miner saw that broadcast and something clicked. Sullivan might just be the host he was looking for. Ironically, considering Sullivan's soon to be notorious nervousness, the thing that impressed him most was how calm and polished Sullivan was.

That is an interesting point. People who saw Sullivan speak at dinners and other functions—before he came down with arteriosclerosis in 1966—always remember two things about him. One was the ease and grace with which he spoke and the other was his fantastic memory for detail. Ironically, it was those two qualities that failed to communicate themselves on screen, and these apparent deficiencies came to be satirized most cruelly by friends and critics alike.

Miner launched a major campaign to convince his superiors at CBS that a Broadway columnist could be transformed into a television star. There was a lot of skepticism but nobody seemed to have a better plan and Miner was given the green light.

Sullivan, apparently, was blissfully ignorant of all this haggling over his fate. He once recounted how he got the news:

"I was playing the Roxy Theatre with the Harvest Moon winners when Marlo Lewis charged through the dressing room door. 'Do you want to do a TV show for CBS?' he gasped, tired from sprinting up the stairs. 'I hope you do, Ed, because I brought Tony Miner with me.' And that's how it all started."

Sullivan had met Lewis a few months earlier when he had been asked to serve as chairman of the Heart Drive in New York City and was trying to figure out how to persuade local disc jockeys to provide some free plugs for the drive. Monica Lewis, a blonde singer on his bill at the Roxy, suggested that he ask her brother, Marlo, and his wife, Minna Bess, both of whom worked for the Blaine-Thompson advertising agency, to help. They did and Sullivan was impressed with their ability to get things done. Marlo had been involved in the production of a radio show called *Luncheon at Sardi's* and when the TV show became a reality Ed asked Lewis to join him as co-producer.

This is the story the way Worthington Miner remembers it and the way Sullivan wrote it a few years later. Marlo Lewis disputes this version and says that he sold the idea of the show to CBS, that Tony Miner had nothing to do with the show until it was already on the air, and that Ed concocted the "Miner-discovered-me" story because Tony was a big wheel at CBS and Ed wanted to get his support.

In any event, Ed and Marlo frantically scurried around trying to line up talent for an opening show. Miner was not happy with the first results. As he told Max Wilk in *The Golden Age of Television*, "He brought me back a very limp list of tired performers—stale acts that were second-string all the way down the line. Ed couldn't talk any of the top headliners around into coming on the show." Miner says he explained to Sullivan that he missed the point, which was to find "new" talent.

For Sullivan and Lewis, it was back to the drawing board. And in a hurry, too. Only a couple of weeks remained until air time.

Things were just as hectic at CBS. The network had bought the old Maxine Elliott theater and was frantically remaking it into a television studio. This involved tearing out the entire orchestra floor, building a control room, putting in camera cables and power lines and lights, and installing sound equipment. Miraculously, the theater was finished on time.

On June 20, 1948, *Toast of the Town* premiered. No kinescope of that first program exists, but according to eyewitness accounts and a look at the guest list, it was "rilly-big."

On the recommendation of his daughter Betty, Sullivan had lined up a young Italian-American crooner who had recently teamed with a second-rate Borscht belt comic. Together they were terrific. Dean Martin and Jerry Lewis were their names; they walked away with $100 apiece and were delighted to get it. Dancer Kathryn Lee got $75 and pianist Eugene List got $100. That effectively used up the talent budget of $375 and Sullivan and Lewis had $1,000 with which to pay Ray Bloch and his orchestra, six members of the June Taylor Dancers who were masquerading as the "Toastettes," and assorted technical personnel.

Fortunately, they were able to round up some "volunteers." Richard Rogers and Oscar Hammerstein dropped by to say hello. Monica Lewis, Marlo's sister, sang for free. In a stroke of genius, Sullivan also decided to add some "newsmakers," people who were not performers but had been in the papers for one reason or another in recent weeks. An heroic New York City fireman named John Kokoman was added, along with Ruby Goldstein, who had refereed the Joe Louis-Jersey Joe Walcott fight a week earlier. Sullivan had a little ring set up and interviewed Goldstein leaning against the ropes. It was the show's first "set."

There was a second young comedy team booked for the first show but they didn't make it to opening night. Jim Kirkwood and Lee Goodman were a couple of young actors who had put together a comedy routine and won a talent contest at a club called Number One Fifth Avenue. For their prize, they were booked at the club, between Faye Emerson and Nancy Andrews. Their humor was sophisticated and New Yorkish and they built up a following rather quickly. Sullivan saw them in the club and they got lots of laughs so he booked them for the first TV broadcast.

Jim Kirkwood, now the successful author of *P. S. Your Cat Is Dead,* and *A Chorus Line,* remembers the day of the show very well.

"This was supposed to be the biggest break you could get in show business," Kirkwood says. "Lee and I called everybody we had ever known in our lives and told them we'd be on. Our big bit was a version of the Saber Dance done to the tune of 'Night and Day.' We wore these kitchen strainers for fencing masks. We didn't know what the hell we were doing but we were cute and energetic. Our other piece of material was a takeoff of 'Tea for Two' that I stole from Danny Kaye."

Although they were only a little younger, Kirkwood and Goodman idolized Martin and Lewis, who had already built up a big following with club appearances in New York and New Jersey.

"We got to the theater about nine thirty on that Sunday morning and we walked in and there were Dean and Jerry rehearsing. They weren't just good, they were socko. I said, 'Jesus, Lee, are *they* on the show, too?' I knew we were dead.

"Well, they finished and we went up and did our little bit. There was a kind of stunned silence and I saw this confab going on in the back and somebody from MCA came up and suggested that maybe we should just do the Saber Dance number. So the day wore on and we rehearsed it a few more times and there was another confab and the guy from MCA came back up and said, 'You know, Ed feels that Dean and Jerry are pretty strong.' 'No shit,' I said. The upshot was they wanted us to trim the number to something like three minutes and two seconds and we just couldn't do it. So we weren't on and we were crushed. How could we face our friends?"

Kirkwood and Goodman did make the show several times after that, but it was never easy.

"We were a constant frustration for Ed, I think," Kirkwood says. "He would come and see us at a club like the Blue Angel and we'd be killing them and he'd invite us to the show and it just didn't seem to work. Our humor was very New York, I mean, Jesus, we carried our props in two boxes, one labeled Hammacher and the other Schlemmer.

"I probably shouldn't tell this but it's the strongest memory I have of him. We had developed this bit which was a takeoff on those *Reader's Digest* headlines that scare you into buying the magazine: 'America's Newest Health Menace—Zippers'; 'Are America's Tennis Balls Underfuzzed?'; 'Do the Duke and Duchess?' Those were the clean ones. Most of them were off-color. Ed loved it and wanted us to come on the show with it. I told him that we really couldn't do most of the bit on TV but he said not to worry, it would be great.

"I knew we couldn't do it on the show and I checked with the CBS censor who agreed and I thought that was the end of it. The next time we were scheduled to be on, he came into the theater and we were rehearsing another routine. He charged up to the stage and grabbed me by the shirt: 'You little bastard,' he said, 'I told you to do the *Reader's Digest* bit.' I said, 'Ed, we can't do most of it. I checked.' He said, 'Forget that. Do you have music for that bit?' I said, 'Sure, but I left it at home.' He literally dragged me to the door and said, 'You little prick, you get the fuck over there and bring that music back, and he kicked me, hard, right in the ass. I was embarrassed, of course, but we went ahead and did the show—and the one minute we could do of the *Reader's Digest* routine—because he would have ruined us. As it was, he introduced us by saying, 'You probably won't understand these next two guys but they're real big on the New York cafe circuit and if you've lived in New York you'd like them as much as I do.' Talk about damning with faint praise. Anyway, my feelings about him were always an odd mixture of affection—he wanted so badly for us to be a hit on his show—and anger."

Kirkwood and Goodman did pretty well without much television, though. They played the best clubs in New York and London before Jim departed for a feature role in the serial *Valiant Lady,* followed by immediate success as a writer with his first novel *There Must Be a Pony.* Lee Goodman is still a busy actor in New York. Their first rejection on the Sullivan show seems light years away.

The first show was seen on six stations. The competition in New York was two feature films, *Gentleman from Dixie* and *Jimmy Steps Out.* NBC had Senator Robert Taft in a convention interview program from Philadelphia.

It was, in retrospect, a marvelous bit of booking and it set the tone for the next twenty-three years. The show was a "column" and each performer or newsmaker was an "item." Sullivan simply introduced the "item" and departed the stage as quickly as possible. As in his column, he always opened with the big news first. He figured he had only a few seconds to grab the viewer's attention before that viewer went on to another channel. Open big. Keep it clean. Always have something for the kids. It was the winning formula and, miracles of miracles, Sullivan discovered it his first time out.

Looking at early kinescopes of the show, one is struck by how little the show changed over the years in terms of pacing and style. Sullivan got older and his hair got thinner, but his television show was one of those incredible conceptions that are born whole.

Sullivan's "amateurishness" embarrassed executives at CBS, critics at first ignored the show and hoped it would go away, but the public loved it. Almost overnight Sullivan was the one thing he had always most wanted to be, a star, a bona fide celebrity, a person who commanded respect. People recognized him, said hello, asked for his autograph. He was the king of Sunday night.

There are those who say that Sullivan was lucky, that he fell into a good thing. Had he come along later, when television was more sophisticated and competition keener, the theory goes, he would have failed. That may be true.

But this is also true: Sullivan's success was no accident. He had spent his entire life preparing for this moment and, once it arrived, nothing or nobody was going to take it away from him.

Toast of the Town
1948–1952

Toast of the Town was a hit with the public right from the beginning. This was before ratings surveys, however, and information about who was watching, or how many, was difficult to come by. There was little response from the press either.

The day after the premiere, Ed and Marlo rushed out to get the papers only to discover that the critics had ignored them completely. Not even Sullivan's own paper, the *Daily News,* had bothered to review it. None of the rival papers were too keen on plugging a competing columnist and the *Daily News* had its own reasons for ignoring him. The paper had just opened its own TV station in New York and had made a last ditch effort to get Sullivan and his show. His commitment to CBS was already established, however, and there was nothing Sullivan could have done, if indeed he had wanted to. That didn't stop the *Daily News* management from being a little annoyed about the whole affair.

Sullivan and Lewis couldn't afford to waste too much effort

worrying about the slight. They were sailing through uncharted waters and there were reefs everywhere. From the beginning, in terms of the many different kinds of things it attempted to bring to the home screen, the Sullivan show was the most ambitious on the air.

There were staff problems which had to be resolved within a matter of weeks. Sullivan was unhappy with the June Taylor dancers, who were known as the "Toastettes," and he had not yet found a director who could swing with his conception of a footloose, spontaneous approach to television. This was 1948, and there weren't that many people around with television experience.

Sullivan hired John Wray as choreographer and soon realized that what he had really found was the ideal director. Wray was unflappable. His father, also named John Wray, had been a prominent stage and screen actor during the 1930s, appearing in over forty pictures in a ten-year span, including a remarkable performance in *All Quiet on the Western Front*. Young John had grown up in show business. He knew more about all aspects of theater than anyone else connected with the show, including Sullivan. If Ed wanted to switch the bicycling monkeys and the girl singer in the middle of the program, no problem.

"Johnny had a great ability to roll with the punches," an associate remembers fondly. Oddly enough, it may have been precisely Wray's cool that led to his break with Sullivan in 1962, after thirteen years as director, but we'll get to that in due course.

Once Wray had stepped into the director's chair, his wife Rae MacGregor, a marvelous dancer, became lead dancer on the show and handled the choreography.

Another important addition to the Sullivan team was Mark Leddy, an ex-vaudeville agent who was the undisputed king of the novelty act. Describe any act between consenting adults, monkeys or elephants and Leddy could immediately name it—and its agent. He, too, was able to adapt to Sullivan's highly volatile personality.

32

"There was never any formula," Leddy said. "The only thing you could be sure of was the first act opened the show."

Leddy remained with the show almost until it folded and was one of Sullivan's closest associates. A major problem, right from the beginning, was convincing Sullivan that animals could not be reasoned with.

"I found this monkey act once," he says. "Just terrific. Their trainer didn't want to do the show, but I kept after him and finally he agreed. He wanted an awful lot of money, though, and he made me promise that they would get eight minutes. I mentioned it to Ed and he said, sure, sure, no problem. We got them and sure enough the day of the show I get to the studio and Ed has them down for four minutes. He had forgotten all about it. I said 'Ed, we promised this guy eight minutes. It takes them that long to do their act. See that monkey on the bicycle there? He's been trained to go around six times.' Ed just looked at me as if I were crazy. Then he said with infinite patience. 'Tell him to only go around three times.'"

The monkey act in question, incidentally, was the Marquis Chimps and they were among the most popular acts ever to appear on the show.

This incident, and others like it, once caused Leddy to confide to author Jim Bishop: "You wanna know the day Christ died? It was on the Sullivan show and Ed gave him three minutes."

John Wray remembers another incident with animals that might have ended with real trouble.

"Clyde Beatty was the only trainer around then who worked both lions and tigers together," Wray said. "We rehearsed the thing and Ed saw it and everything was fine. About halfway through the act, while we were on the air, he decided he had seen enough. God knows why. Anyway, he sent word back to the control room that he was cutting the act and that I should come to him in the audience. He would do a commercial from out there while the stagehands struck the stage—no easy feat to tear down all those cages and things in just a few seconds.

33

Well, he gives Beatty the wrap and the poor man starts trying to finish in a hurry. Animals are very sensitive to changes in routine and these cats started getting a little worked up. We had no sooner cut to Ed in the audience when all hell broke loose on stage. The lions are pounding the shit out of the tigers. Beatty is beating them with chairs and whips and trying to get them back into their cages. The roar is so loud you can't hear a word Ed is saying. Finally, though, Beatty gets the cats back into their cages and the stagehands get the set down. Unfortunately, they didn't have time to sweep the stage. The next act is a sort of romantic dance team and they're doing a routine which involves a lot of floor work. Well, these cats had crapped all over the goddam stage and you could see these poor kids sliding all over the place."

It was an animal act that was to bring the show its first lawsuit. The routine called for a team of greyhounds to do their tricks, then run out the stage door and onto a truck that held their cages. Greyhounds are a particularly temperamental lot who don't much care for other dogs.

Just as the greyhounds raced out the door, a lady happened by, walking her poodle. The greyhounds ripped the poodle to shreds. It cost Ed and Marlo a few bucks to placate the distraught owner.

On yet another occasion, Sullivan booked a man-wrestles-bear act. At the end of the act, the bear always got an ice cream cone as his payoff. Someone thought it would be cute if Sullivan gave the bear his ice cream.

Everything went along fine during the program. The trainer and the bear were wrestling on a mat at center stage. Toward the end of the routine, an aide handed Sullivan the ice cream. As he sometimes did, Sullivan strayed away from his mark and downstage to get a better view of the act. Meanwhile, the cone started to drip so he absentmindedly started licking it.

At that moment, the bear looked up and did a double take. There was a man eating *his* ice cream. The bear flung the trainer to the floor and made a lunge toward Sullivan. The trainer's wife, armed with a pistol, ran to intercept the bear. Fortunately, before she could shoot, the trainer tackled the bear from the rear. For months after that, Sullivan stayed pretty much where he was supposed to.

Sullivan's problems with the unpredictability of live television were nothing compared to his problems with the network. Although his show was a hit in the ratings, such as they were at the time, from the first night on, CBS was sensitive to criticism of Sullivan as a performer. When Emerson Radio, the first sponsor, bowed out after thirteen weeks, CBS began offering *Toast* to other potential sponsors "with or without Sullivan."

Until his dying day, Sullivan never forgave CBS management for that slight.

When a critic finally did get around to reviewing the show, Sullivan might well have wished nobody had done him a favor. John Crosby, writing in the *New York Herald-Tribune,* had this to say on December 31, 1948:

> One of the small but vexing questions confronting anyone in this area with a television set is: "Why is Ed Sullivan on it every Sunday night?" If the set owner has been properly conditioned by soap opera, he is likely to add: "Why? Why? Why?" It's in all respects a darn hard question, almost a jackpot question, and it seems to baffle Mr. Sullivan as much as anyone else.
>
> The program is *Toast of the Town,* a CBS enterprise (8 P.M. Sundays), an hour-long variety show and sometimes a very good one. After a few opening bars of music, Mr. Sullivan, who is introduced as a nationally syndicated columnist, wanders out on the stage, his eyes fixed on the ceiling as if imploring the help of God, and begins to talk about his "very good friends." Sullivan's very good friends

35

include virtually every one in show business, several of whom are waiting in the wings to perform their specialties.

One of them—let's say Connee Boswell, who was on the show last Sunday—then comes on stage and the pair of them, Sullivan and Boswell, discuss how enormously fond of each other they are, how profoundly each admires the work of the other and how wonderful it is to be able to meet on this wonderful show in front of this wonderful audience. The entertainer usually hints to the audience that, without the help of Ed Sullivan, he or she would still be slinging hash on Eighth Avenue. Miss Boswell then goes on with her song.

"Let's have a nice hand for that wonderful girl," says the nationally syndicated columnist when the act is over. "Connee, come out and take a bow. How do you like that, eh? Wasn't that wonderful?"

Sullivan at this point halts operations to introduce some of his very dear friends in the audience. These may include Barney Ross, Barry Wood, James Dunn, Jerry Colonna, or Bob Hope. If the dear friends are show people, Mr. Sullivan may request them, with rather steely insistence, to come up and amuse the folks. Mr. Hope, one of the highest paid entertainers in the world, obliged with evident reluctance, and his opening words to Mr. S. were: "The first thing I'd like to discuss with you is money." Later when Jerry Colonna was persuaded (bludgeoned would be a more apt description) into joining Mr. Hope, the comedian remarked wryly: "Remember, this is for nothing."

Not all entertainers are as eminent as Bob Hope, and naturally there are many who haven't the courage to make such wisecracks about a man who has a nationally syndicated column at his disposal. One entertainer I know who gets from $1,500 to $2,000 a week in night clubs was talked into doing his cherished routines—he only has three—on the show for $55. Mr. Sullivan is a persuasive fellow.

If he has any other qualifications for the job, they're not visible on my small screen. Sullivan has been helplessly fascinated by show business for years. He has been in vaudeville, on the radio, and now on television. He remains totally innocent of any of the tricks of stage presence, and it seems clear by now that his talents lie elsewhere.

Otherwise, *Toast of the Town* ranges in quality from very good to very bad, depending on the entertainers. In this respect it differs from NBC's opposite number, *Texaco Star Theatre*. Milton Berle, the emcee of that show, can transform indifferent vaudeville acts into something pretty special simply by appearing in them. On *Toast of the Town*, the entertainers are on their own. The good ones like Connee Boswell, who was introduced as the possessor of "one of the most thrilling voices of our generation," a slightly excessive estimate; or Hazel Scott or Dean Martin and Jerry Lewis or Kathryn Lee or Monica Lewis—all of whom have appeared on the show—don't need any help.

The CBS show is marked by an elegance that the *Texaco Star Theatre* hasn't and doesn't seem to want. You find upper-class night-club acts on *Toast of the Town*, where *Star Theatre* sticks pretty closely to good old rowdy vaudeville. Also, *Toast of the Town* opens with a chorus number—usually pretty terrible but a step in the right direction—and closes with a big, rousing finale. It could be a wonderful Sunday night program—and sometimes it is.

But what is Ed Sullivan doing there?

Sullivan was livid. He suspected that Walter Winchell was really the force behind Crosby's attack. He fired a letter back to the *Herald-Tribune:*

Your review of my CBS *Toast of the Town* television show, in last Sunday's issue, is in error on so many points that I must challenge it.

You object to "Ed Sullivan's predilection for introducing his friends in the audience," on the grounds that it "slows up the show." If the introductions were of nondescript characters, or of my grocer or butcher, you'd be on firm ground, but when the introductions bring to the television camera the retired undefeated heavyweight champion, Joe Louis; the manager of the Brooklyn Dodgers, Leo Durocher; Tin Pan Alley's Richard Rodgers, I seriously question that your reaction is shared by the video audience.

Perhaps a newspaper man is bored by seeing these celebs, but to the television public, names make news and faces make news. The mail proves that you are wrong, if proof were needed, and the studio audience underscored it.

From every survey we have been able to make, the CBS *Toast of the Town* has the biggest audience in television and the most enthusiastic. C. Bennett Larson, director of television for the Philadelphia *Bulletin* and Station WCAU, has written to CBS: "Sullivan's *Toast of the Town* has advanced television by five years." Oscar Hammerstein II, a rather experienced hand in show business, has expressed his delighted amazement at our progress in a completely new medium and specifically praised "the professional polish, the pacing of the show and the high entertainment value." Eddie Cantor, after seeing the show on a television set, said that we were so far ahead of any program he's seen that he was dumbfounded at the potentialities of a medium he had disregarded.

Your conclusions are at such variance to the expressions of expert showmen, and so opposed to public reaction, that I feel very strongly that you are in error.

So much for the over-all show.

As to your opinion of me as master of ceremonies, I won't challenge that, because difference of opinion makes horse racing.

However, I do feel that when you compare me with a Milton Berle, you misunderstand my position on our show. They wanted a working newspaper man, sufficiently versed in show business, to nominate acts that could live up to a *Toast of the Town* designation. As it is a Sunday show, they wanted a certain measure of dignity and restraint, rather than a vain attempt to work with acrobats, tumblers, etcetera, which Berle does brilliantly.

Ed Sullivan

Sullivan's problems were not just with the critics, however. The Associated Actors and Artists of America called him in to explain his wage practices on the show and to question him on allegations that he was using the influence of his column to pressure acts to appear for virtually nothing.

Sullivan told a negotiating committee that as soon as a sustaining scale was established for television, he and CBS would pay the stipulated amount, but meanwhile he believed he was paying the highest sustaining rate in video. He said that until an official rate was adopted by the unions, he would continue to pay acts at the rate of $50, $75, and $100 for an appearance.

He categorically denied that he had pressured anyone to appear on the show and pointed out that headliners like Phil

Silvers and Sid Caesar had refused to go on with him.

The unions were particularly wary of columnists-turned-broadcasters. Some years before Louella Parsons had been involved in a scandal in which, the unions claimed, she coerced celebrities to appear on her radio program *Hollywood Hotel.*

Ultimately, the unions adopted rules that prohibited TV shows from using talent for less than the acts would normally get for a nightclub appearance. "Talk" shows were exempt.

The money issue was to lead to a highly publicized falling out with Frank Sinatra. In the spring of 1955, Sullivan made a deal for $32,000 with Sam Goldwyn to show thirty minutes of the movie *Guys and Dolls,* which starred Sinatra, Marlon Brando, and Jean Simmons. Goldwyn thought the deal would help push the picture and Sullivan wanted the box-office names.

Sinatra was incensed and said he wouldn't approve the deal unless Sullivan paid him $25,000.

Until then, the two men had always been friends of a sort. Sinatra had appeared in Sullivan's war-relief shows in the 1940s and when a number of columnists—most notably Westbrook Pegler—attacked Sinatra for sitting out the war and for his alleged connections to Lucky Luciano, Sullivan mounted a vigorous defense. Sinatra even sent Sullivan a wristwatch with a note that said: "Ed, you can have my last drop of blood."

About the same time as the *Guys and Dolls* flap, the Screen Actors Guild issued a ruling to prevent newspaper personalities from using movie stars on TV without pay. Sullivan felt he had to respond and he took the back pages of both the Hollywood *Reporter* and *Variety* to respond in an open letter to SAG president Walter Pidgeon:

Dear Walter:

Let us waive the important fact that the SAG ruling actually was directed at other columnists, not me. Let us waive, for the moment, the fact that I haven't talked to Sinatra in some years; and let us overlook the fact that Sinatra, regularly trounced by us when he becomes part of the rival network's "spectacular," hardly qualifies as an impartial or disinterested witness.

What I particularly resent is Sinatra's reckless charge that *Toast* does not pay performers. To date we have paid out over $5,000,000 in salaries and, incidentally, rendered substantial benefits to motion pictures, motion-picture artists, studios, and theater operators.

If Sam Goldwyn approached Sinatra, that hardly is my concern or problem. Certainly, I never approached Sinatra. My negotiations with Mr. Goldwyn involved an offer by me to pay a substantial sum of money, $32,000 covering studio technical costs, to represent, on film, thirty minutes of *Guys and Dolls* as an exclusive preview.

Sincerely,
Ed Sullivan

P.S. Aside to Frankie Boy—Never mind that tremulous 1947 offer: "Ed, you can have my last drop of blood."

Four days later, Sinatra ran his answer in the same papers: "Dear Ed, You're sick. Frankie. P.S. Sick, sick, sick!"

The feud was short-lived, however. A few months later, Sullivan was involved in a serious automobile accident. The first person to volunteer to guest-host—for free—was Frank Sinatra.

It's a matter of opinion, of course, but Sullivan really wasn't that bad a performer. Consider the January 16, 1949 show:

Fanfare.

"Emerson Radio—the world's largest maker of home radios—presents The Emerson Show *Toast of the Town* with the nationally syndicated columnist, Ed Sullivan."

The "Toastettes" appear and do a cornball dance routine which ends with Radio City Music Hall high kicks.

Sullivan wanders out on stage, sharp as always in a double-breasted suit, his hair slicked back in the greasy style of the day and parted on the right. "Good evening, ladies and gentlemen,

41

and welcome to another Emerson *Toast of the Town* Show. We're going to open the show tonight, but first I want to welcome into the coaxial cable network for the Emerson Toast of the Town—Chicago, Cleveland, St. Louis, and all the western cities that are coming in tonight for the first time on a direct wire. I would also like to welcome WOIC in Washington."

Sullivan then introduces a young comedian named Wally Boeg, his words bouncing across the vaster reaches of the coaxial network like flat rocks skimming across water. "Command performance . . . President of France . . . Princess Margaret. . . ."

Wally Boeg, it turns out, is a guy who blows up balloons and twists them into animals and other shapes while keeping up a string of witty patter. He is quite marvelous, actually. (This routine of Boeg's was a major influence on Steve Martin, one of the top comics of the 1970s.)

"Isn't he wonderful," Sullivan says, when Boeg is finished. "That really is a fine act."

Sullivan then introduces "a new girl star of Broadway . . . comedienne Jean Carroll." She is not as funny as Wally Boeg.

A live commercial follows, delivered by Ray Morgan. "Ray is going to demonstrate how easy it is to *Emersonize* your home."

Back to Sullivan. "Last time I played the Roxy . . . young ventriloquist . . . Bob Evans and Jerry O'Leary."

Bob and Jerry do their bit. Jerry is the dummy, but his lips move less than Bob's.

"Wonderful, Bob," Sullivan says. "You know, the other day in my column I wrote that I thought the most lovely young star on Broadway was Nanette Fabray. Please welcome this young . . . starlet."

Nanette sings "Mr. Right." She didn't sing any better then than now.

"I want to tell you," Sullivan says, embracing Fabray after the song, "this is a little trouper. She has laryngitis and wasn't supposed to be here, but she came and performed anyway."

42

The audience applauds.

"Now sitting out there . . . Lee Schubert . . . who built this theater. I participated in the writing of his biography . . . I will be taking orders after the show." The audience laughs. The biography was never published.

Sullivan then engages in some fairly witty banter with professional heckler Patsy Flick, an old friend from vaudeville days.

Ray Morgan does another commercial, this one for the Emerson Model 611 TV set which has a nine-inch screen and can be had for $269.50.

"Now here's a man I predict is going to be a greater star on TV than he was on radio . . . Rudy Vallee."

Rudy appears wearing a cowboy hat. He sings a couple of songs. Clearly he is not going to be big on TV.

Sullivan then says that Rudy has hidden talents in the area of ventriloquism. He suggests that Rudy bring his female dummy over to meet Bob Evans's Jerry O'Leary. It is a strange spot. Rudy whispers something to Bob Evans. Evans says, in a voice audible to everybody listening, "We know our lines. You just learn yours, that's all." For once, his lips didn't move.

Sullivan then says a few nice words about cab drivers and signs off. On this particular show, at least, he has been the best performer in the house.

After Lincoln-Mercury signed on as sponsor and rescued him from CBS's kiss of death, Sullivan threw himself into their cause with as much energy and passion as he had ever attacked anything in his life. In his mind, at least, the Ford Motor Company stood between him and filing clippings at the *Daily News* morgue.

Sullivan began traveling around the country making appearances on behalf of the car company. He chalked up thousands of air miles and became its "ambassador" to the world. The ratings of *Toast of the Town* had begun to soar and his ulcer began to flare.

His major problem with his sponsor was a delicate one. Many of the Lincoln-Mercury dealers around the country—not just in the South—thought he was entirely too friendly with black performers. It was an issue on which Sullivan never backed down.

He once had a high Ford official thrown out of the theater when the man suggested that he stop booking so many black acts.

When a dealer in Cleveland said to him, "We realize that you got to have niggers on your show, but do you have to put your arm around them?" Sullivan had to be physically restrained from beating the man to a pulp.

Sullivan believed fervently that talent was the ultimate measure of a person. Race and color were incidental. He would have booked Martians if they had had a hit record or could tap dance well.

Sullivan's appreciation of black talent went all the way back to his days on the New York *Graphic* when he once scouted New York for a place where the great black basketball teams of that period could play (he found it—an armory). During the 1940s, he had tried to revive a black revue called *Harlem Cavalcade* without much success. His great and good friend was Bill "Bojangles" Robinson. When "Bojangles" died, it was Sullivan who paid for the funeral.

It took courage to continue giving a platform to black performers in the face of his sponsor's opposition, but Sullivan did it. Ethel Waters. Lena Horne. Nat "King" Cole. They, and many others, were first presented to the TV viewing public through Sullivan's show.

There was another matter, though, on which Sullivan was not so courageous. In context, it was not such an evil thing—nothing that others weren't doing even more vindictively—but it was wrong and haunted Sullivan for many years to come.

Late in 1949 Sullivan booked dancer Paul Draper for a *Toast of the Town* appearance in January 1950. An appearance by

Draper and harmonica player Larry Adler in Greenwich, Connecticut, had recently touched off a flurry of letter-writing by a Mrs. Hester McCullough of Greenwich. Aided by Hearst columnist Igor Cassini, who wrote as "Cholly Knickerbocker," Mrs. McCullough, who had for some time been interested in the hunt for subversives—"I guess you might say I was always on the lookout for them"—demanded that the Greenwich appearance be cancelled. She called Draper and Adler "pro-communist in sympathy" and said that any such person "should be treated as a traitor." Draper and Adler issued a statement, carried by the Associated Press, saying that they were not and never had been communists, members of the Communist Party, pro-communists, or traitors, and that they owed and gave allegiance "solely to the United States under the Constitution." They filed suit against Mrs. McCullough. The Greenwich appearance proceeded without incident. Sullivan booked Draper for *Toast of the Town.*

But Hearst columnists and various newsletters took up the battle again and demanded that Ford cancel the scheduled appearance.

Ford and its advertising agency, Kenyon and Eckhardt, held nervous meetings and decided to go ahead. The possibility of a lawsuit was a factor in the decision.

The columnist and newsletter, continuing their protests, managed to elicit angry letters and telegrams in response to the telecast. As in most such campaigns, there were duplicates. Clusters came from the same post office. Most letters echoed published attacks. Eight percent said that "leftists" and "pinks" should be sent back to Stalin. Thirteen per cent said that communism threatened Western civilization. The mail caused enough trouble to produce further meet ings between sponsor and agency, in which it was decided that Sullivan should send a letter to William B. Lewis, president of Kenyon and Eckhardt—a letter which was drafted for the purpose by public relations counsel. It also served as a press release.

January 25, 1950

Dear Bill:

I am deeply distressed to find out that some people were offended by the appearance, on Sunday's *Toast of the Town* television show, of a performer whose political beliefs are a matter of controversy. That is most unfortunate. You know how bitterly opposed I am to communism and all it stands for. You also know how strongly I would oppose having the program used as a political forum, directly or indirectly.

After all, the whole point of the *Toast of the Town* is to entertain people, not offend them. . . . If anybody has taken offense, it is the last thing I wanted or anticipated, and I am sorry.

I just want *Toast of the Town* to be the best show on television. I know that's what you and the sponsor want, too. Tell everybody to tune in again next Sunday night, and if I can get in a plug, it will be a great show—better than ever.

Sincerely,
Ed Sullivan

Kenyon and Eckhardt promised to do everything possible to prevent other such incidents.

Draper found he could no longer earn a living in the United States and went to live in Europe. Sullivan began to turn more and more to Theodore Kirkpatrick of *Counterattack* for guidance. Liaison between Sullivan and Kirkpatrick became "extremely close." In case of doubt about any artist, Sullivan checked with Kirkpatrick. If the entertainer seemed to have "explaining to do," and Sullivan still wanted to use him, he would get Kirkpatrick and the artist together to see if things could be ironed out. Sullivan seemed anxious to report this closeness. He told his column readers on June 21, 1950:

Kirkpatrick has sat in my living room on several occasions and listened attentively to performers eager to secure a

certification of loyalty. On some occasions, after interviewing them, he has given them the green light; on other
occasions, he has told them Veterans' organizations will
insist on further proof.

Sullivan said that *Counterattack* was doing "a magnificent
American job."

When Kirkpatrick was about to publish his infamous *Red
Channels: The Report of Communist Influence in Radio and
Television,* he gave Sullivan an advance copy. Sullivan de-
scribed it in his column as a "bombshell."

That it was. And, in fact, it was the beginning of the end of
Kirkpatrick's influence because his list of suspected subversives
was made up of 151 of the most talented and admired people in
the broadcast industry.

One might ask why Sullivan allowed himself to be duped by
Kirkpatrick. For one thing, the Cold War was ablaze at the
time. Sabers were rattling in all corners of the globe. Sullivan
had been too young for World War I and too old for World War
II. Like many men who have not served in the military during
war periods, Sullivan was sensitive about it and insecure about
his "patriotism." He did not want to be accused of not having
done his part. Despite the fact that he was to become the first
man to present many great Soviet acts to the American public,
Sullivan remained a fervent anti-communist.

"Sullivan thought he was being extremely patriotic, I
suppose," Larry Adler told me during one of his rare New York
appearances last year. The undisputed king of the mouth organ
is nearing seventy but is as feisty as ever and his brilliance as a
musician has not diminished. "I remember we once had a long,
long meeting at the Delmonico. He held out the promise of an
appearance on his show if I would go before the House Un-
American Activities Committee and name names. Well, I
wanted to be on the show; everybody did. It was the difference
between working and not working. But, for me anyway, the
price was just too high.

"I must say that Ed was not as vicious to me in his column as were Winchell and the Hearst columnists. Maybe it was because I used to go out to Staten Island with him and play in the hospital out there. I remember the last time I saw him. It was about 1952 and I was living in Europe because I couldn't get work over here. Ed and his wife came to see me at the China Theatre in Stockholm and he took me to dinner after the show. It was kind of courageous of him, I suppose, being seen in public with a notorious 'commie' like me. I remember he told me that he thought I had had a raw deal.

"I think he was under the influence of Bishop Sheen and Cardinal Spellman a lot during this period. He really, honestly, thought he was being a good American."

Toast of the Town
1952–1955

The critics kept hoping Sullivan would simply go away but week by week the audience for *Toast of the Town* continued to grow. By 1952, thirty-seven of the 108 television stations then broadcasting carried the show to some 13,600,000 viewers a week. More people were acquiring television sets daily and come Sunday they were likely to be tuned to CBS at 8 P.M. Nothing the other networks could throw up against Sullivan seemed to matter much. People just couldn't believe that they were getting for free what they used to have to pay money for in the vaudeville houses.

The operation of the show was firmly fixed from the beginning. Although Ed and Marlo Lewis shared the title "co-producer," there was never any doubt in anyone's mind that it was Sullivan's show and that he was the boss. Although he declined to be interviewed for this book, Lewis did say that he and Sullivan were "partners." That may be true, but the available evidence suggests it was not an equal partnership. Ed, with Carmine Santullo manning the telephone, did all the booking for the show. Marlo found out who was going to be on when Ed got around to calling and telling him. If Lewis resented this arrangement, nobody ever heard him complain.

This is not to diminish Lewis's impact on the show. He had an enormous influence over the years, particularly in leading Sullivan into experiments with the higher arts. It is fairly safe to assume that the show's early presentation of opera, of dancers like Margot Fonteyn and, later, the Moiseyev dancers, and of pianists like Van Cliburn, were partly the result of Marlo's efforts.

As an executive producer at CBS, Lewis also played an important role in the development of such shows as *The Phil Silvers Show,* and in handling stars like Jack Paar and Jackie Gleason. Lewis was everything that Sullivan was not. He had come from the sort of family background that seems mainly to exist in fairy tales. Marlo's father, Leon, had been a child prodigy who at the age of fourteen was hustled off to Vienna to study piano. Leon had then become a noted concert pianist, had scored silent pictures for symphony orchestras, and later became musical director of CBS Radio. He was also a composer, whose best known work is "The Israeli Suite."

Marlo's mother, Jessica, was no less involved in the arts. She had been a member of Ben Greet's Shakespearean Players and for years sang leading roles with the Chicago Opera Company.

By the age of seven, Marlo himself had conducted a symphony orchestra and knew Charlie Chaplin, Douglas Fairbanks, Jr., and Mary Pickford.

"I didn't learn about show business playing tennis at UCLA," Marlo said recently, a cryptic remark that will become clearer later in the story.

Despite the great disparity in their backgrounds, Sullivan and Lewis were very close. Marlo's sister, Monica, says her brother was "devoted" to Sullivan and that their relationship was like "father-son." Indeed, Marlo was thirteen years younger than Sullivan.

His job on the Sullivan program was to get the show ready, to get rehearsal halls for dancers and singers, to see that singers got their arrangements together—working with orchestra leader Ray Bloch—to see that the scenic designers got their work done. In short, his function was to mount the show. Sullivan never really saw it until the dress rehearsal on Sundays. In those days, he used to ad lib his opening remarks and introductions. Looking at old tapes of the show, it's easy to believe they weren't on cue cards.

At the dress rehearsal, and before the actual show, Sullivan would wander out onstage to "warm up" the audience himself. "Hi, there," he would say, "Anybody here from out-of-town?" Most of the audience would raise their hands. "No wonder us New Yorkers can't get tickets for the show." It always got a laugh. Sullivan would ask everybody to smile and have a good time, "not for me but for those people back home who paid for you to get here."

What the dress rehearsal audience didn't realize was that they were about to take part in a deadly serious piece of business. How they reacted would determine the shape of the real show that night. A comic who got no laughs at the dress rehearsal would find that he was no longer on the agenda for that evening. A juggler who had come all the way from Europe and whose act didn't seem to fit in with the rest of the show would find himself paid his fee and sent home wondering what had gone wrong. A singer with a song that Sullivan, or more properly, the dress rehearsal audience, didn't like would find himself quickly learning the lyrics to a new song. Sullivan's say in the matter was final and in those days he seldom changed his mind.

Sullivan would almost always rearrange the order of performers, order cuts in some acts, time added to others. Opinion varies among the people who worked there in those days as to whether these changes actually worked to the benefit of the show or whether they were simply Sullivan demonstrating that he was the boss.

Talent coordinator Mark Leddy was a believer. "That was

Ed's real talent," he says. "He could take a show that was shit vaudeville in the afternoon and reshape it into a pretty good show by the evening."

John Wray, who was director in those days, isn't so sure, particularly about Sullivan's use of the studio audience as a gauge of what the viewing public might enjoy. "He never once stopped to ask himself what kind of people come to television shows, anyway," Wray says. "I think he relied much too much on what that audience thought. I saw some good performers get chased off the show because a bunch of tourists whose feet hurt didn't react enough."

Sullivan's faith in a live audience as the ultimate measure of an act was unshakable, however. And—as many a young comic found out—he was extremely protective of his audience.

One of those who discovered this truth the hard way was a sensational young comic named Woody Allen who was just beginning to emerge in the mid-1960s. Allen managed to run afoul of Sullivan on his first appearance on the show.

"I did the Sunday morning run-through and, of course, you don't do the same material at the run-through that you're going to do on the show, but there was a full audience. So, because it was not on the air, I didn't censor myself at all. I'm not particularly dirty anyway but by the rather clinical standards of *The Ed Sullivan Show* I appeared to him as absolutely filthy.

"And he got me in his office afterward and just hit the ceiling. He was enraged. He told me that it was because of me that this whole Vietnam thing was happening and how dare I talk like that to an audience and it's offensive. He apologized to the audience for me.

"And I was sitting there and I had that kind of thing that goes through your mind under these circumstances of deciding right then and there if you want to say something really nasty back to him. And my impulse was to say something terrible to him, but I didn't. I said, 'Gee, I'm sorry. I didn't realize you felt that way about it,' and that was it.

"And it subsided and I did the show that night and for the

rest of my life . . . for the rest of his life . . . he was wonderful to me. I mean, absolutely wonderful. He went out of his way to be nice to me . . . to print nice things about me. If I ran into him on the street, he carried on like a relative in the family. And I think what happened was, the old guilt got him. You know, by not going with my impulse to be nasty, but by playing a real shrinking violet at the time, he was so overcome with guilt by his yelling at me that as the years went by he couldn't have been more wonderful." The incident obviously made a strong impression on Allen who recently recounted it on *The Dick Cavett Show.*

Allen was not the only performer who was subjected to one of Sullivan's outbursts and who later found Ed anxious to make amends. Once Nat "King" Cole, whom Sullivan had championed at a time when it was unpopular to do so, was scheduled for an appearance and he wanted to sing a new song which was his latest record release. Sullivan wanted him to sing some of his classics. There was a falling-out and Cole did not appear. Later, when Sullivan learned that Cole was seriously ill, he announced it on the air, touching off a torrent of some 600,000 telegrams and letters from well-wishers.

Still, Sullivan ran the show with an iron hand. Sid Caesar and Imogene Coca, who were very big at the time, did a bit which got no laughs during rehearsal. He dropped them without a second thought. Dinah Shore wouldn't sing the material he had selected for her. She was off the show and was never invited back.

Jim Kirkwood remembers being backstage when Pearl Bailey's agent called to say that Pearl was running a fever of 103 and just couldn't make the show that night. Sullivan turned a bright crimson and screamed into the phone: "You tell Pearlie Mae that she'd better get her ass over here." She did.

Sometimes bumping an act off the show could have nearly disastrous consequences. Sullivan, on one of his periodic forays to Europe, saw a hefty woman who held the title "Strongest Woman in Britain," and booked her for the show. She was to get $500 for the appearance, plus her transportation and hotel costs.

On the Sunday she was scheduled to appear, the early acts ran long and the strong lady got bumped.

"Not to worry," Sullivan told his giant friend. "You're marvelous and we want you on the show. You're opening the show next week. None of this nonsense. We'll give you another $500 and another week at the Belvedere Hotel."

Sure enough, throughout her week and right up until ten minutes before show time, the strong lady was scheduled to open the show. Then something else came up, and she was shifted once more to the end. And, as fate would have it, the show ran long again and the strong lady didn't get on.

It took five CBS security guards to prevent her from breaking Sullivan in half and to wrestle her out of the studio.

For the agents who booked talent on the show, the dress rehearsal was an experience never to be forgotten. Agents waited backstage to hear the good or bad word in an area the production people called "the wailing wall."

Sullivan would be sitting on his stool just offstage and agents dreaded to hear him call their names. Marty Kummer, who booked talent on the show for MCA on a week-to-week basis, was one.

"Marty Kummer."

Marty would trot up to the stool.

"What is this, Kummer, amateur night in Dixie? Get that schmuck off my stage."

The good agents, and Marty was one of them, took their defeats graciously and went back to the drawing board. Those who put up too much of a fight found the going even tougher next time.

Some of the really clever ones learned to appeal to Ed's vanity. More than once an untalented female singer-dancer got on the show because an agent whispered in Sullivan's ear that the girl really had the hots for him.

One of the most brilliant manipulations, though, was pulled

off by an agent named Joe Wolfson, from William Morris. Wolfson knew that Sullivan was annoyed because his show was frequently compared, seldom kindly, to Max Liebman's *Your Show of Shows*. Forget that *Your Show* rehearsed five days a week and the Sullivan show, in those days, was thrown together with chewing gum and bailing wire on Sundays. Sullivan was still envious. He was particularly upset when Liebman signed a comic named Dick Shawn, who was the bright young face of 1952, to a one-year contract amidst much fanfare.

The fact of the matter was that Shawn really didn't fit in too well and at the end of the year, Liebman was not going to renew his option. Wolfson, who was Shawn's agent, took a chance that Sullivan hadn't heard the news.

"Listen, Ed," Wolfson said. "There's a situation here. I don't think Liebman realizes that Dick's option is up next week. If we act now, I think maybe you can steal him away."

"Hey, that's great," Sullivan said. "How much is the kid getting?"

Wolfson allowed that he wasn't getting all that much now, but with the option he was going to be getting top price. Wolfson figured that Ed should pay Shawn his top price of $7,500 a show.

Sullivan agreed and booked Shawn for ten appearances.

That fall Shawn came on the first show and did his classic bit called "Masses on the Cold, Cold Ground." It was brilliant and the audience loved it.

A month later, Shawn was back with his second-best bit and it went over a little less well.

The third appearance was a bomb.

Before the fourth appearance, Sullivan said, "Perhaps we should have a little chat about your material."

By appearance five, Sullivan insisted that Shawn use some of the Sullivan show writers.

By appearance six, Sullivan suggested that he, himself, would write the damn bit.

Sullivan apparently never realized that he had been conned, because Wolfson remained in his good graces. Actually, Sullivan liked agents a great deal more than he liked their clients, and he spent time with them. Marty Kummer remembers one particularly intimate moment with Sullivan.

"We were sitting in Ed's dressing room—Mark Leddy and Ed and me—one night after the show. It had been a real good show, but Ed was feeling down because the audience really hadn't reacted much. We were getting a little drunk and Ed said, 'I want to see young faces out there next week. These old people don't know what's happening.' Mark Leddy, who was already about a hundred, shook his head and said, 'Yeah, Ed, you're right. It was those same old farts who killed vaudeville.'"

The final two hours before air time were always chaotic and there are those who believed that Sullivan, always a gambling man, liked it that way. Like many newspapermen, he needed the pressure of a deadline to do his best work.

He also seemed to understand that his most important contribution to the future well-being of the show was based not on what he did on Sunday night but rather what he did on Monday, Tuesday, and sometimes Wednesday. By 1953, Sullivan had already logged more than 250,000 miles around the country in his role as "Ambassador" for Lincoln-Mercury. He had appeared before a crowd of 92,000 in Philadelphia and had had breakfast with an entire Texas town. He had floated down the Mississippi on the Royal Barge of the Memphis Cotton Carnival and landed on the Boston Common in a helicopter. One summer, from Paris, he sent postcards to every Lincoln-Mercury dealer in the country, all beginning "Dear Joe" or "Dear Bob," or whatever the dealer's name happened to be. He was like a politician, gathering goodwill for future use.

In 1951, Sullivan decided it was time to move away a bit from standard vaudeville fare and *Toast of the Town* launched a series of television biographies, fifteen in all over the next two seasons.

The programs were ambitious, and well-done, and were almost certainly the first television "spectaculars."

The real impetus for the shows was the fierce competition NBC was throwing up against Sullivan. *The Colgate Comedy Hour,* with its rotating format of major comics like Eddie Cantor, Bob Hope, Martin and Lewis, Abbott and Costello, and Donald O'Connor, was beginning to make a dent in Sullivan's seemingly invincible lead in the ratings. Ford had not yet had its better idea, but Sullivan did, with the help of Marlo Lewis and John Wray.

A listing of those "biographies" and their guests is interesting because they represent the cream of American entertainment at that moment.

Oscar Hammerstein Story—presented September 9 and 16, 1951. With Oscar Hammerstein II, Robert Merrill, Mimi Benzell, Bill Tabbert, Nanci Crompton, Charles Winninger, Carol Bruce, Gertrude Lawrence, Dolores Gray, Lisa Kirk, Muriel Rahn, Sandra Deel, Richard Rodgers, Ray Bramley, Allen Shane, George Hall, David Burns, Judson Laire, Wally Cox, Lena Horne.

Robert E. Sherwood Story—November 18, 1951. On stage were Robert E. Sherwood, Helen Hayes, James Mason, Pamela Kellino, Alfred Lunt (he made his TV debut on the show), Raymond Massey.

Bea Lillie Story—February 3, 1952. With Beatrice Lillie, Les Compagnons de la Chanson, Reginald Gardiner, Richard Rodgers, Constance Carpenter.

George White's Scandals—February 17, 1952. With George White, Harry Richman, Richard Hayes, Smith and Dale,

Toni Arden, Frances Williams, Costello Twins, Danny Hoctor.

Cole Porter Story—February 24 and March 2, 1952. With Cole Porter, Monty Woolley, Mimi Benzell, Dolores Gray, William Gaxton, Brian Sullivan, Pierre De Angelo, Helen Wood, Jane Froman, Roberta Peters, Lisa Kirk, Nanci Crompton.

Richard Rodgers Story—June 15 and 22, 1952. With Jane Froman, Vivienne Segal, William Gaxton, Lisa Kirk, Richard Hayes, Bill Lawrence, Cindy Lord, Sinclair and Spaulding, Richard Rodgers, Celeste Holm, Yul Brynner, Martha Wright, Ray Middleton, Juanita Hall, John Raitt, Cloris Leachman, Philadelphia Choir.

ASCAP Story—September 28 and October 5, 1952. With Patricia Marand, Clark Dennis, Joe Howard, Jack Norworth, Harry Tierney, Ernie Rose, Alice Lawler, Maude Nugent, Mabel Wayne, Vaughn Monroe, Lauritz Melchior, Les Compagnons de la Chanson, Fritzi Scheff, W. C. Handy, Ray Henderson, Dorothy Fields.

A Night at Sophie Tucker's House—October 19, 1952. With Sophie Tucker, Rex Harrison, Lilli Palmer, The Ink Spots, Ronny Graham, Harry Mimmo.

Bert Lahr Story—November 9, 1952. With Bert Lahr, Edith Piaf, Delta Rhythm Boys, Harry Mimmo.

Sam Goldwyn Story—December 7, 1952. With (on film) Gary Cooper, Teresa Wright, Babe Ruth, Eddie Cantor, Dana Andrews, Frederic March, Harold Russell, Laurence Olivier, Merle Oberon, Danny Kaye, Ronald Colman, Vilma Banky, Geraldine Farrar, Will Rogers, Samuel Goldwyn.

Walt Disney Story—February 8, 1953. With Snow White and the Seven Dwarfs, The Three Little Pigs, Peter Pan, Mickey Mouse, Pinocchio, The Little Train.

Josh Logan Story—May 17, 1952. With Joshua Logan, Leland Hayward, Ralph Meeker, Janice Rule, Kim Stanley, Scott Jackson, Eileen Heckart, Ruth McDevitt, Gary Merrill, Paul Newman, Janet Blair, Juanita Hall, Irma Sandre, Sheila Bond, Jack Cassidy, Patricia Marand, James Stewart (on film).

In addition to bringing to the home screen for the first time dozens of performers who had never been there before, the "biographies" produced one of television's most memorable and, indeed, important moments.

Joshua Logan, who directed *Bus Stop, Picnic,* and *South Pacific* and wrote *Mister Roberts,* had waged a long and private— at least to the general public—battle with mental illness. He had told Sullivan several weeks before the broadcast that he wanted to talk about his mental breakdown and his stay in a sanitarium and to tell the audience that mental illnesses can be cured. Mental illness was not a topic that people talked about much in those days and Logan's friends—and Sullivan himself—discouraged him from doing so.

In the middle of the show, Sullivan found Logan backstage looking grim and unhappy. Logan told him that he wished he had gone through with his determination to talk about his breakdown. In one of those spur-of-the-moment changes of mood that Sullivan was prone to, he asked Logan if he still wanted to do so.

Sullivan had the music cut and went out on stage and introduced Logan.

"This has been gratifying to my ego, but it's not important," Logan began. "As it happens, I do have one important thing to tell the country, and I'll tell it quickly. I never got any of the awards I've won until I'd been committed to a mental hospital and released from it. I tell you this because the world is suffering from tension, with the result that many people are crippled by mental breakdowns. The old way of treating them was to hide them in the garden house when people came to visit in warm weather, or lock them up in the attic in winter. You don't have to do either any more. A lot of people who are disturbed mentally can be cured. There is no reason why they should go through life bearing a stigma because they have once been mental patients. The proudest memory of my life is that although I had been in the theater a good many years, I never won the Pulitzer Prize until after I had been in the sanitarium."

A hush fell over the theater, followed by a tremendous burst of applause. For weeks after, telegrams and letters poured in praising Logan's courage. A taboo subject had finally been brought out into the open and it was as if a giant blanket of guilt had been removed from the nation's shoulders. Sullivan was to remember it always as the show's finest moment. The irony is: it almost didn't happen.

The year 1952 was a landmark one for Sullivan. *Toast of the Town* celebrated its fifth anniversary—an incredible 260 consecutive Sundays of live television—and his daughter, Betty, got married.

Her husband was Robert Precht, a handsome young Navy lieutenant (JG), whose family lived in San Diego. They had met at UCLA where Betty majored in English and he in international relations. Precht had later transferred to Berkeley but they had continued their relationship.

Precht and Sullivan had not gotten on well together at first. Betty introduced Bob to her parents over dinner at Chasen's, a fancy and well-known L.A. restaurant.

"I was very naive and unsophisticated, I guess," Precht recalls. "California was a long way removed from the world of Broadway gossip columnists and I was only sort of aware that he had something to do with television. I was very interested in politics at the time and I was upset at the loyalty oaths that teachers were being forced to sign and at Richard Nixon's witchhunt. I guess I launched into a soliloquy about that because Ed suddenly said, 'Well, if you're that upset, why the hell don't you stop talking about it and do something?' That brought me up short. I remember that Betty and her mother were both upset and embarrassed. All in all, it was not a good first meeting."

Things got better, though. Every summer the Sullivans would come to California for a month and Betty would leave her sorority house and move in with them at the Beverly Hills Hotel. Bob owned a 1938 Chevy that was falling apart. When he came to visit, he would park it around the block to avoid the embarrassment of having one of the hotel car boys park it.

Gradually, Sullivan began to respect his future son-in-law. Young Precht was not—as Sullivan was to learn—without a certain iron will of his own. He could hardly have guessed that this young man, whose background and experiences were so different from his own, whose interests were so far removed from entertainment and show business, would eventually be the one who provided the first real challenge to the absolute authority Sullivan held over his television show. Seven years after his marriage to Betty Sullivan in 1952, Bob Precht was to become producer of *The Ed Sullivan Show* and things would never be quite the same again.

The Boy Singer

One of the most spectacular of Sullivan's many feuds took place in 1953 when he ran headlong into another broadcasting titan named Arthur Godfrey. The issue was a pleasant, gregarious boy singer from Brooklyn named Julius La Rosa.

La Rosa was a Godfrey "discovery," quite possibly the most popular of the fiery redhead's many finds. Julius had been a deckhand on the aircraft carrier *Pensacola* when Godfrey, a pilot with good government connections, decided he'd like to learn to land on a carrier. One night while Godfrey was staying aboard the *Pensacola,* one of La Rosa's pals sneaked into his room and said, "Listen, I got this friend with a great voice, see. Sounds just like Sinatra. You ought to give him a shot." Godfrey listened and liked what he heard. La Rosa was not the greatest singer in the world but he was good and he came across as an incredibly nice guy, with his boyish good looks and teddy bear personality. Godfrey invited him to come to New York during one of his leaves from the ship to appear on his radio program.

La Rosa did and was an instant hit. When Julius got out of the Navy, Godfrey made him a regular on his five-day-a-week radio show and on his Wednesday TV show, *Arthur Godfrey and His Friends*.

"I was just a dumb kid, twenty-three-years-old, and I'd never had a singing lesson in my life," says La Rosa, now approaching fifty but as boyish-looking as ever. "I really wasn't prepared for what was about to happen to me."

What happened was Julie became incredibly popular. He started getting five or six thousand letters a week. Girls wanted to marry him. Mothers wanted to adopt him. He made a recording of "Anywhere I Wander" that sold 750,000 copies. Young Julie started getting a swelled head and his mentor started having second thoughts.

For his fifth anniversay show on June 14, 1953, Sullivan spotlighted all the "little Godfreys"—La Rosa, the Mariners, Frank Parker, Haleloke, LuAnn Simms, Janette Davis, the McGuire Sisters, and Tony Marvin—and annoyed Godfrey no end by paying them considerably more than they were getting for their regular stints.

Four months after that appearance, the La Rosa-Godfrey troubles came to a head. There were a series of incidents. Godfrey had ordered all his people to take ballet lessons for some peculiar reason or another. Julie failed to show up for most of them as, indeed, did nearly all of the other performers. Still worse, La Rosa hired himself an agent. To Godfrey this was a monumental act of ingratitude. He didn't like agents and there was an unwritten rule that his performers shouldn't have them.

One Monday morning in September, Godfrey brought La Rosa on the show just before closing. When he had finished, Godfrey said, "Thank you, Julie. And that, folks, was Julie's swan song."

Thus La Rosa was fired on the air, before an audience of millions.

One of those listeners was Marlo Lewis who immediately got

on the phone to Sullivan. Sullivan was later to write:

"I phoned Frank Barone, La Rosa's lawyer. 'What the hell goes, Frank?' I asked. 'Is what I've just heard from Marlo on the level or. . . .'

"'The kid's fired,' he interrupted. 'Wait a minute, he's just come into the office. He's crying, Ed.' I could hear him call to La Rosa: 'Take it easy, Julie, take it easy.'

"'Tell La Rosa to stop crying, Frank. I'll use him on our show next Sunday night and I'll give him a six-show deal.'

"'Julie,' yelled Frank. 'Ed's willing to take you on his show. Here, talk to him quick.'

"I gave him $3,000 a week, far more than he ever got on the Godfrey show, and it was the cheapest and best buy I ever made."

And, indeed, it was that. Because of Godfrey's prominence and his strange way of firing La Rosa, and because La Rosa was so well-liked, the story hit page one from Maine to California.

The next Sunday night, immediately after he was introduced, Sullivan said "I know what you are waiting for—ladies and gentlemen, Julius La Rosa." The audience went wild. La Rosa, obviously choked up, sang "Eh, Cumpari" and "I'm Sitting on Top of the World."

The next morning's Trendex gave the Sullivan show a 47.9 to the competition's 11.2. It was one of the biggest wins in the history of the Sullivan show.

La Rosa laughs at the memory now. "I was so naive," he says. "I thought Sullivan was having me on because he liked the way I sang or the way I combed my hair. I didn't realize that it had nothing to do with me personally. I was the hot news that week."

La Rosa made thirteen appearances on the show that first year, a fact that he now regrets. "I wasn't ready," he says. "I should have said 'Let me go to the mountains, play some clubs, get some experience, learn to sing.' The exposure I got on that show hurt me in the long run. People got tired of me, I guess, after awhile."

La Rosa's singing career went into a decline during the Sixties and he spent several years as a disc jockey in New York. That career is over now and he's now singing again. Better than ever, as a matter of fact.

Oddly enough, neither Godfrey nor Sullivan ever revealed the major reason La Rosa was fired. Julie was having an affair, a serious one, with one of the McGuire Sisters. She was married and her husband was a Korean War hero. For the jingoistic Godfrey, that was too much.

It would have been too much for Sullivan, too, if the affair had become public, but it remained a secret.

"He was very nice to me about that," La Rosa says. "I thought I wanted to get married and he even arranged for me to talk to a bishop about it. He was a tough man, but he could be very kind."

Certainly, Sullivan never missed a chance to throw a dagger at Godfrey in the years that followed.

When Godfrey fired Marion Marlowe the following year, Sullivan booked her for ten appearances. As he almost always did whenever he made long-term commitments, he began to regret it after about the fourth appearance. Over two years passed and finally Marlowe was down to the last appearance on her contract. It was an Easter Show and Sullivan decided that Marion would open with a big dance number and close the show singing "Ave Maria." Right before show time, though, he told Marlowe that she would have to do both numbers back-to-back. Marlowe made the altogether reasonable observation that she was wearing a very low-cut gown with a split up the leg for the dance number and somehow that didn't seem too appropriate for the "Ave Maria."

Sullivan nodded, then spotted a priest sitting among the early arrivers for the show. "Father, would you come here a moment, please," he said.

The startled priest made his way up to the stage.

"Do you know Miss Marlowe?" Sullivan said.

"No, I haven't had the pleasure," the priest answered.

"Tell me, father, how do you think she looks?"

"Oh, I think she's beautiful," the priest said.

"See, kid, I told you you got nothing to worry about," Sullivan said.

So Marion did the dance number, followed by the "Ave Maria."

The next morning, Sullivan got a phone call from one of his sisters in Port Chester. "Who was that whore who sang the 'Ave' last night?" the voice on the other end demanded.

"You're absolutely right," Sullivan said. "She'll never be on *my* show again."

In 1954, after Godfrey was involved in a celebrated "buzzing" of an airport control tower, Sullivan wrote one of the most scathing columns of his life:

On Nov. 1, 1949, the control tower at Washington, D.C., National Airport ordered the flier of a P-38 to make a left turn and circle the field. He disobeyed, violated the traffic pattern, crashed into an Eastern Airlines DC-4, and killed 55 people, including veteran airline pilot Captain Charles Hazelton, Tammany leader Mike Kennedy, New York cartoonist Helen E. Hokinson, Massachusetts Representative George J. Bates, and 51 others.

So the flippancies of Arthur Godfrey, in answering charges of reckless operation of his DC-3, taking off from Teterboro Airport are shocking. Godfrey is 50, hardly the age for a hot-rodder.

The Teterboro control-tower log gives a sinister pattern to Godfrey's flippancies. I asked the CAA if, following the hairbreadth escape of control-tower personnel, Godfrey had radioed an apology or explanation to the men he had endangered.

'The control tower contacted Godfrey immediately,' said the CAA spokesman. 'They asked him if the plane was out of control, or in trouble.'

What did Godfrey reply?

'No, that's just a normal Teterboro takeoff,' said Godfrey.

That contemptuous reply to the control tower best illustrates Godfrey's major weakness, his inability to apologize. But this time it has caught him in the backfire. . . . Godfrey is sensational on a TV screen. But there's no place for sensationalism in flying. That is for the birds.

The two old tigers never spoke to each other again after that.

The Mimic

Will Jordan could hardly have guessed what sort of monster he was going to create or that the monster would eventually consume him. In those days—the late Forties and early Fifties—Jordan was simply another of the many young Jewish comics who hung out at Hanson's, a sleazy combination luncheonette and drugstore on Broadway at 47th Street. On a good day at Hanson's you might have seen Lenny Bruce, often glassy-eyed even then, Jack Roy (who later changed his name to Rodney Dangerfield), Buddy Hackett, and Jordan all crammed into the same booth, practicing new bits on each other, trying to outdo each other with schtick. You probably wouldn't have recognized them, though, because they weren't that famous yet.

The successful comics, the Milton Berles and the Jack Leonards, took their business up the street to Lindy's. Hanson's was schmucksville, a hangout for losers and people about whom a judgment had yet to be made. In truth, the silverware wasn't that much cleaner at Lindy's and the signed photographs of forgotten hoofers were just as fly-specked, but the members of both clubhouses were painfully aware of the implied social order.

Although he was accepted by the group, Jordan remained something of an outsider. For one thing, he was an "impressionist" which to a hard-core stand-up comic meant a man who was not funny and who had to resort to the cheap trick of mimicry to get a laugh. Not that most of the boys at Hanson's didn't have a few impressions as part of their repertoire. Impressions were always popular and a little Cagney here, a little Bogie there, could mean the difference between getting a job and not. That was the other thing about Jordan. He had an amazing talent for finding work. To an unemployed comedian nothing is so distasteful as another member of his ranks who has a gig.

Jordan was, by far, the best impressionist of the group. He simply had the knack. And the incredible thing about it was, he didn't really look like anybody. If you had put Jordan in a line-up with five guys off the street the day after one of his Sullivan appearances, the chances are good that few people who had seen him would have been able to pick him out.

What Jordan had, and still has, was a very analytical approach to features and bone structure, a talent for makeup, and a face as mobile as Silly Putty.

He could be funny, too, and like most of the regulars he was often surprised to hear Bruce repeating on stage—in slightly revised fashion—something he, Jordan, had said at one of the cowboy sessions at Hanson's.

Jordan was working small clubs around New York and would frequently do a short impression of Sullivan as part of his act. It had a few of the body gestures that would later characterize his advanced Sullivan impression—just a few lines here and there, a throw-away, really.

Steve Allen liked Jordan and would often have him on his local show on WCBS and would never fail to ask him to do Sullivan. Unfortunately, Allen was not yet a household name himself and those shows had little impact on Jordan's career.

The big local program in those days belonged to Harry Hirschfeld and in February 1953 Jordan finally landed a booking on it.

A couple of days before the scheduled appearance, he ran into Joe Moore, a Sullivan friend and unofficial "scout," at Hanson's. He mentioned his good fortune and Moore promised to have the boss watch.

What Jordan didn't know was that Sullivan and his production people had been looking for some way to demonstrate that old stone-face was not as uptight as he appeared on camera. By having him react to a young comic impersonating him, they reasoned that Sullivan would be able to create a more endearing image. (Actually, Sullivan was aware that he appeared wooden and tense on television almost from the first and always had some sort of crutch to show what a nice guy he really was. Within a few weeks of his opening show in 1948 he hired Patsy Flick, a professional heckler and old friend from the vaudeville days, to sit in the audience and razz him in a heavy Yiddish dialect. Patsy would say clever things like "Did you look dat vay vhen you vere alive?" or "Come on, Soloman, for God's sake, smile. It makes you look sexy." After the mimic gimmick wore off, Sullivan turned to the Italian puppet Topo Gigo as a way of demonstrating his personal warmth.)

Although Sullivan was, in fact, a very egotistical man, he was concerned lest his audience sense it. As he coyly told Pete Martin in a 1958 *Saturday Evening Post* interview: "A lot of fans feel that my walk is an expression of personal conceit. They say, 'It makes you look smug and stuck-up.' When I read that I started putting Will Jordan, the professional mimic, on my show to do imitations of me. I thought it would indicate to the viewers that I am so far removed from excessive egotism that I enjoy being joshed about the way I handle my body."

Sullivan was right, of course; the Jordan impression did eventually make him appear less cocky. Not the first time out, though.

Jordan's first appearance in March 1953 was a moderate

disaster. Perhaps he was afraid to satirize Sullivan too much on his own show, or maybe he was just scared at being on national television but his act went nowhere. To make matters worse, the show that night was opposite a Bob Hope special and a Martin and Lewis *Colgate Comedy Hour* and took one of the worst ratings beatings in its history.

Convinced that he had blown a big chance, Jordan returned to the club circuit. He didn't give up on the Sullivan impression though and he continued to refine the bit, adding the herky-jerky body gestures. The idea for his version of Sullivan's walk came from watching mechanical ducks in a shooting gallery. He also added the stammering forgetfulness. "Now, let's rilly hear it for old what's-her-name," Jordan would say, and audiences would roar.

Columnist Hy Gardner caught Jordan's act one night in early 1954 at a club called La Vie en Rose. He thought it was very funny and he sent a note to Sullivan saying so. Sullivan replied that he had had Jordan on the show before and that it was nothing special but if Hy thought the kid was good he'd give him another shot.

Jordan was feeling a little feistier this time around. His career had taken a dramatic upswing. He was opening for Eddie Fisher, then the hottest singer in the business, at the Coconut Grove in Los Angeles, and getting a lot of laughs. Opening night had gone so well that Eddie Cantor, obstensibly on stage to introduce Fisher, had practically done a testimonial. Even dour Walter Winchell, who wouldn't have bought Jordan an egg cream back at Hanson's, gave Jordan a "You done good, kid" sign afterwards.

Jordan flew in from the coast—a big deal for a Hanson's cowboy—to do the show. Believing this time that he had nothing to lose, he launched into the Sullivan bit with a vengeance.

"Tonight on our rilly big sheew," he said, cracking his knuckles, popping his eyes, and swiveling his body as if the head were permanently locked in a face forward position, "we have 702 Polish dentists who will be out here in a few moments doing their marvelous extractions. . . ." The audience howled. The camera cut to Sullivan who was bent over double with laughter. The audience screamed so long and loud, in fact, that Jordan almost couldn't get another line out.

Now the fact of the matter is, Sullivan had never said a "rilly big sheew" in exactly that way in his life but it was one of those brilliant flashes of inspiration that sound so right that they transcend simple reality. Sullivan couldn't even get it right after Jordan invented the phrase. One night a year later he came out and said "As Will Jordan might say, tonight we have a *truly* big sheew."

"I was feeling pretty pleased with myself," Jordan admits. "Suddenly everybody knew who I was. I got back to the coast and found out I'd been booked into the Mocambo, one of the best clubs out there. I really figured I had it made."

There is a hint of a sardonic smile on Jordan's face as he recalls that period of his life. I should have knocked on wood, it says.

"A couple of weeks later I flipped on the Sullivan show and there was Robert Wagner, the movie star, introducing a protege a black kid named Arnold Dover. And Dover does my act. He doesn't even change the lines. I was furious but I figured, okay, this guy isn't a big name so don't worry about it," Jordan says.

What Jordan hadn't yet realized was that there was going to be a flood and he was going to be Johnstown.

"I started seeing Jack Carter in the audience and I thought, gee, isn't this terrific, a famous comedian come to see little old me," Jordan says. "About a week later, I found out why. He came up to me after a show and you could see he was just bursting over. He launched into an impression of me impersonating Sullivan. He just couldn't hold it in. He had to show me. I think that's when I first sensed how things were going to be."

After Carter came Jordan's old friend Jackie Mason and after him John Byner whose impression was, perhaps, the cleverest of all. They all had something in common, though. They were impersonating Will Jordan. True, each added a few new wrinkles and some new lines but Jordan had set the tone, established a motif. There were times when even Sullivan appeared to be impersonating Jordan.

Sullivan continued to book Jordan, more than twenty times in all, but he also continued to book the others and what galled Jordan most was they were all getting paid more than he got because they were headliners.

Over the next several years, Jordan saw Sullivan frequently enough to run afoul of his celebrated temper on three separate occasions.

The first explosion came in 1955 when Jordan went on tour with Sullivan and a group of other performers. They played theaters and high school gyms in little towns across the country. People came to see Sullivan. The acts were pretty much incidental, although Jordan always wowed them with his impressions. One night in San Francisco, Jordan—who was bored with doing the same routines over and over—dropped in a few Japanese bits. He didn't realize that a lot of the audience were Nisei—Japanese-Americans who had remained loyal to the U.S. during World War II—or that Sullivan was passionate on the subject. Ed hit the roof.

"Don't you ever change a line again without asking me," he said, poking Jordan in the ribs with his index finger.

The second incident involved Jordan's recording of "Bye, Bye Love," a big hit for the Everly Brothers, which he had made using Sullivan's voice. Sullivan himself had done a satiric record with the Kirby Stone Four, so Jordan figured he wouldn't mind. He was wrong.

"Ed stopped speaking to me or booking me," Jordan says. "I finally got hold of him and asked him why he didn't like the record. He said because of all the awful things I had him saying in it. I said 'What do you mean, Ed? The part about the Polish

74

dentists? I've done all those things on your show.' He said 'No, not that. Those awful things . . . bye, bye love, bye bye happiness.' I said 'Ed, those are the words of the song. It's a hit record.' He says, 'You didn't make them up?' I said, 'No, those are the words of the song.' He said, 'Oh' and that was the end of that episode."

Jordan's final falling out with Sullivan was the most serious. Will was in a Toronto nightclub when the comic on stage invited him to come up and do Sullivan. Jordan declined vigorously and someone in the audience reported to Sullivan that Jordan had said, "If I do that one more time, I'm going to vomit." Jordan swears he didn't say that. It took months of delicate negotiation and a trip up to Sullivan's apartment with his then-agent to convince Sullivan that he had heard wrong.

By 1962, Jordan could not—as they say in show business— get arrested. He was too identified with the Sullivan impression. Although he did other people, talent coordinators always said, "Oh, he's the guy who does Sullivan." Lots of other comics—most notably Jordan's former friend and protege Rich Little—did Sullivan just as well.

"I thought I was finished," Jordan says. "My hair fell out, William Morris dropped me, and I lost a girl I was in love with."

Fortunately, Jordan was able to pull himself together. He became his own agent. He got hair transplants. He found other girls and, most importantly, he discovered the extremely lucrative field of trade shows and industrials. He admits he is sometimes a little bitter, though.

During the past couple of years, Jordan's Sullivan impression has made something of a comeback. Will played Sullivan in the Broadway production of *Elvis—The Legend Lives* and in the film *I Wanna Hold Your Hand*.

"I really don't blame Ed, I suppose," he says. "He could have stopped those other people from stealing my act but he didn't. Then, maybe I just didn't make the bit grow as much as I should have. The last time I saw him we did a commercial together. It was shortly before he died. He was old and tired and he couldn't remember his lines—he only had two or three. It was sad. He was a complex man, though. I'm not sure anybody really understood him."

Part II

Sullivan, The Man

The Port Chester Kid

If there is a secret to the longevity of the Sullivan show and its exalted place in the history of American television, that secret lies—at least in part—in the personality and background of the man himself. Although Sullivan the performer embarrassed his network and worried his sponsors, he entered the new medium a seasoned show business veteran. The circumstances of his life, its many divergent paths, seem to have prepared him, almost singularly, for what was clearly to become his life's role.

Ed Sullivan was five years old when his family moved to Port Chester, a sleepy factory town sandwiched between Long Island Sound and the Connecticut border, twenty-six miles north of New York City. His sister, Helen, who was eight, and brother Charles, who was seven, held him up to the train window so he could get his first glimpse of a cow. The rail car was drab olive green with hard wicker seats and was pulled by a Baldwin 4–4–0 steam engine—property of the New Haven line of the New York Central Railroad Company. The cow was the first any of the Sullivan children had ever seen.

The Sullivans were moving from 114th Street in the Harlem section of Manhattan. Harlem was still mostly white and middle-class in those days—which was 1906—but it was already starting to change. The city, as a whole, was crowded and dirty, more populous then than now, the population of some slum neighborhoods even denser than that of Bombay— more than one thousand human beings per acre.

Edward Vincent Sullivan was born on September 28, 1901, a strong husky child. His twin brother, Daniel, was puny and weak and died at about nine months of age. When another child, Elizabeth, died shortly after birth, her mother—for whom she was named—laid down the law: We are leaving this city before it kills us all.

Peter Arthur Sullivan, head of the household, was not averse to that decision. He was really a farmer at heart and had only come to the city in the first place because of his work. He was a minor official at the Customs House, a political patronage job that paid twelve dollars a week. None of the children (two more daughters were born in Port Chester) ever knew exactly what it was that he did there.

Ed's mother, Elizabeth Smith Sullivan, was the perfect Victorian lady. Her family came from that area of New York State north of Utica that Edmund Wilson memorialized in his classic *Upstate*. Her father, Edward—for whom Ed Sullivan was named—was a landholder who had married an Irish squatter's daughter and there was about Elizabeth a certain air of fallen gentility. She was a beautiful woman with long brunette hair, thin wrists and neck, and an impossibly small waist, which was the fashion of the day. She loved to paint and to garden. She died in 1929.

It was a gentle time, the age of ragtime, and life in Port Chester proceeded at a leisurely pace. Liberty Square, the main junction of the town, was lined with watering troughs for horses. Traveling medicine shows and gypsies selling horses would often come there and hawk their wares. The village blacksmith was a busy man. In the fall a big deal for the local

80

kids was to go down to the park at the end of Pearl Street and watch the Model Ts, Packards, and Pierce Arrows zoom by on the Boston Post Road on their way to football games at Yale in New Haven.

There was no television in those days. In England and Russia, various pioneers were busy inventing the bits and pieces of technology that would eventually become television. But to the Sullivans and their neighbors, the possibility that they would someday be able to sit in their living rooms and watch people thousands of miles away was as remote as the notion that somebody might eventually walk on the moon.

The parlor was the entertainment center. On Sundays, relatives would gather around an upright piano and sing such current hits as "O, Promise Me," or "Only a Bird in a Gilded Cage." The Sullivan parlor, like many others of the era, had an aspidistra and a suite of mahogany-stained furniture uphol-stered in velveteen. Gilt frame chromos and engravings hung on the walls. Peter and Elizabeth's bedroom had a gleaming brass double bed with cover and pillow-shams of crocheted lace over a lining of blue sateen.

Because there was no television, people also read books and occasionally talked to each other.

By his early teen-age years, Ed was already showing signs of developing his celebrated temper.

"He had a terrible bout of scarlet fever as a child," his sister, Helen Culyer, recalls, "and after that he suffered terribly from what we today would call sinus trouble. I've always wondered if that might not have had some effect on his disposition. He could be very kind and gentle but he was quick to anger sometimes."

Sullivan drifted into newspapering for a variety of reasons. He loved reading and sports and becoming a reporter seemed a sensible way to stay close to the things he enjoyed. Also, newspapering was pretty much a man's game in those days, an excuse to chase fire engines, hang out with hookers, suspected murderers and known press agents, go looking for bodies in muddy rivers at dawn, and to drink a lot—an occupational hazard of newspapermen, Irish and not.

In school, he had covered sports for the Port Chester *Daily Item* (circulation 3,900) for a dollar a column and after graduation the publisher offered him a regular job at twelve dollars a week. He jumped at the chance. He found, however, that his regular assignments also included police court and three local undertakers.

It was a wonderful time to be a sportswriter and Ed was enjoying his newfound power immensely. This was the Golden Age of Sports, the age of Babe Ruth, Rogers Hornsby, Ty Cobb, Jack Dempsey, Bobby Jones, and Big Bill Tilden. When Babe Ruth played in an exhibition game in Port Chester, Sullivan interviewed him at his hotel. This made him something of a local hero—the man who had actually talked to the Babe. "That Sullivan boy is going places," people would say, and they were right.

In 1922, Sullivan was hired by the New York *Evening Mail* to write scholastic sports. He was soon promoted into the regular sports department and made college-sports editor, with golf and tennis as sidelines.

The *Mail* was staffed by some of the top newspapermen in the business like Rube Goldberg, Mary Margaret McBride, Russell Crouse, and Robert Ripley. The competition was keen but Sullivan was "determined to be the best sportswriter in New York."

His best remembered assignment at the *Mail* was covering a tennis match. In writing up the article he referred to California tennis champion Helen Wills as "little poker face," a nickname that was to stay with her afterward and which was to come back to haunt him since the same phrase was later used to describe his manner as a television host.

Sullivan's salary was seventy-five dollars a week and he spent it lavishly. He bought a Durant automobile and wore hand-tailored suits and custom-made shirts. He had a girl in Port Chester named Alma Burns whom he took out on weekends, and soon he was seen around town in the company of a succession of showgirls. He lived over Billy LaHiff's Tavern on West 48th Street and spent evenings at nightclubs.

His favorite was the Silver Slipper on West 48th where he went almost every evening. Ruby Keeler used to be on the bill and Van and Schenck, and Clayton, Jackson, and Durante. Lou Clayton and Ed would sit up all night and then go out to Flushing for a round of golf first thing in the morning.

In the winter of 1924 the *Mail* sent him to Florida to cover the winter-season sports. His good times ended suddenly when the *Mail* was purchased by the *Sun* and the new publisher decided to kill the paper.

Jobs were scarce in New York so Sullivan settled for a position as sportswriter with the Philadelphia *Ledger* at thirty-five dollars a week. From there he moved back to New York and a series of short-lived jobs writing sports at the morning *World* under George Daley, whom he called a "perfectionist," at the New York *Bulletin,* and at the *Leader,* published by Norman Thomas. For two years he worked on the *Morning Telegraph* until in 1927 Will Gould, sports cartoonist at Bernarr Macfadden's new New York *Graphic,* suggested that Sullivan become a reporter for the Saturday sports-magazine that they were adding to the paper.

The *Graphic* was one of the strangest enterprises in the history of American journalism. Its founder, Bernarr Macfadden, a health enthusiast who often walked the twenty miles from his home to the office barefoot, had made a fortune in sensational magazines, particularly *True Story*. He saw no reason why a newspaper wouldn't do equally well.

In its eight-year history, from 1924 until its more than timely death in 1932, the *Graphic* gave the world Walter Winchell, Ed Sullivan, Louis Sobol, the gossip column, more sex for breakfast than the newspaper-buying public has seen before or since, and a strange aberration called the "composite" photograph. Unable to get a photographer into courtrooms or bedrooms, the *Graphic* took to creating its own versions of incidents, photographing some real-life characters mixed with models standing in for others.

By the time Sullivan arrived at the *Graphic* in 1927, he was a cagey veteran of the newspaper wars and a well-known figure in sporting circles.

Although he was himself only twenty-six, he frequently referred to athletes as "youngsters." An outgoing guy, he made acquaintances easily in those days. He had a habit of immediately getting on a first-name basis with everybody he met, even if it was their first encounter. Around the paper the only person he called "Mr." was Macfadden himself. Like most of the other members of the staff, he found the barefoot owner a trifle weird.

Sullivan's first experience as a promoter came early in his time at the *Graphic*. He organized strong-man tournaments at Webster Hall. They were amazing carnivals of feats of strength. Every known device used to exhibit muscle power and physical endurance was used. Participants arrived carrying huge weights and a strange collection of contraptions. All the strength and sweat, however, did not belong to the competitors alone. It took a considerable amount of both on the part of Sullivan to select the winners. In such a gathering, where human giants with hands like vises that could squeeze the life out of a person in seconds believed the man didn't exist who could top them, the first prize should probably have gone to Sullivan for bravery. Unhappy losers, however, showed great restraint. In quieter moments, some would call on Sullivan at the office to prove he had made a mistake. One tore up his telephone books with easy twists, just to show him. There was another who insisted Sullivan accompany him to 11th Avenue to see him push a freight car with his head.

More pleasant affairs were the *Graphic* sports dinners that Sullivan arranged and emceed—his first attempts at performing. These were notable for the prominence of the guests and the excellence of the entertainment. The *Graphic* might have been held in low esteem, but the dinners were rated as top-notch events. It was at one of these, at the Hotel Astor, that Rudy Vallee introduced the "Maine Stein Song." The roster of guests regularly included Mayor Jimmy Walker, Jack Dempsey, Gene Tunney, Jim Corbett, Babe Ruth, Al Jolson, Gene Sarazen, Red Grange, Sophie Tucker, and many others.

Sullivan also had an opportunity to demonstrate his interest in human rights at the *Graphic*. He managed to get hold of a contract for a basketball game between the University of Georgia and New York University in which NYU agreed to bench their top player for the game because he was Black.

"I wrote then," Sullivan once said in a radio interview, "that if intercollegiate athletics had sunk to that low a level where the gate receipts were the thing . . . where it was more important to make money on a big game in New York than it was to humiliate one man, whether he was an Irish Catholic or a Jew or a Protestant or a Negro, then I suggest that NYU cancel the game and give up basketball."

It was not a popular position to take at the time, but it established a pattern of concern for the plight of black people that Sullivan displayed throughout his lifetime.

By 1930, the *Graphic* was having convulsions. Winchell had departed for sunnier climes at the *Mirror* and managing editor Emile Gauvreau had soon followed. A man named Lee Ellmaker arrived from Philadelphia, where he owned the *News* in partnership with Macfadden, to take over the helm of the *Graphic*.

When Louis Sobol, successor to Winchell, announced that he, too, was leaving, Sullivan reluctantly switched from sports to Broadway.

Sobol wrote a nice farewell column welcoming Sullivan to the Broadway beat and saying some charitable things about his successor's talents. He, like everybody else, was stunned to read Sullivan's first column on June 1, 1931:

I charge the Broadway columnists with defaming the street. I have entered a field of writing that ranks so low

85

that it is difficult to distinguish any one columnist from his road companions. I have entered a field which offers scant competition. The Broadway columnists have lifted themselves to distinction by borrowed gags, gossip that is not always kindly, and keyholes that too often reveal what might better be hidden. Phonies will receive no comfort in this space. To get into this particular column will be a badge of merit and a citation—divorces will not be propagated in this column. . . . In my capacity as drama critic I pledge you of the theater that if I like the show I will say so without any ambiguities of phrasing that might protect my *Variety* box score. . . . With the theater in the doldrums, it means a decisive voice and I promise to supply it.

Reaction to the column was mixed. Winchell and Sobol were furious, both believing the column was aimed directly at them. A lot of people laughed at the sanctimonious tone. Macfadden wanted to know if this guy was serious. He was assured that it was a phase and that no column could exist for long without gossip. Those observers were right.

Three weeks after his noisy debut, Sullivan's column led off with "Grover Cleveland Alexander is back with his wife and off the booze."

In the meantime, Louis Sobol had extracted his own revenge. He dipped his pen in acid to write a column about Sullivan headlined "The Ennui of His Contempt-oraries." He knew Sullivan would be angry, but he could hardly have guessed how much so.

"I was standing in front of a theater at a premiere when I saw him charging toward me," Sobol recalled last year. "He was really angry. 'I'll rip your cock off, you little bastard,' he says. Fortunately, I was able to duck out of the way while some other people held him back." Sobol then and now weighs about a hundred twenty-five pounds soaking wet. The two men were later to become good friends, and, in fact, Sobol and Sullivan alternated in hosting vaudeville shows at Loew's State Theatre.

The *Graphic*, which one obituary described as having "anticipated every news event except its own death," expired on July 7, 1932. Sullivan was one of the survivors. A week before the paper closed shop, he got a call from Captain Joseph Patterson of the *Daily News*, who offered him a job at two hundred dollars a week. It was a pay cut, but he was in no position to be choosy. He took the job and the *News* remained his newspaper affiliation for the rest of his life.

The Women

There is some mystery about when it was exactly that Sullivan met Sylvia Weinstein, the woman who was to become his wife and lifelong companion. One published account reports that they met in 1926 in a nightclub where Sylvia had gone to "celebrate her high school graduation." The latter part is certainly incorrect since Sylvia was twenty-three in 1926, a bit graying to have been a recent high school graduate.

Sullivan himself, in an autobiographical article for *Collier's* and in a tribute written after Sylvia's death, put the date at 1928. He said that one of their first dates was the Harry Wills-Jack Sharkey fight at Ebbets Field in Brooklyn. That fight, however, was in November 1926.

Maybe he simply forgot. Or perhaps he had another, more polite reason for placing the date two years later than it actually was. Until her tragic death in January 1927—more than a year after he met Sylvia—Sullivan was engaged to a woman named Sybil Bauer.

Sybil Bauer was a champion swimmer, the world's first great

backstroker. She won six successive National AAU 100-yard backstroke crowns from 1921 through 1926, won nationals in the 100-meter, 150-yard, and 220-yard backstroke, and was part of a world record national championship freestyle relay team. She won a Gold Medal at the 1924 Olympics in Paris, an event remembered primarily for producing Johnny Weissmuller, who later went on to play Tarzan in the movies.

Sybil was not beautiful. Her nose was a bit too large and her lips were a little thicker than they might have been. But she was pretty and delicate and feminine—the antithesis of what female swimmers are supposed to be.

Sullivan interviewed her at a national event in 1925 and quickly formed a crush. Although Sybil lived in Chicago, he pursued her vigorously. They visited each other regularly and Ed took her home to meet his family in Port Chester. She had a gentle, winning disposition and they were charmed.

Sullivan borrowed money from his sister, Helen, to buy a diamond ring at Black, Starr, and Frost in White Plains and they got engaged. He continued to see Sylvia when Sybil was not in town.

A couple of months after the engagement, Sybil fell from a touring car during a victory parade after her last championship in St. Augustine, Florida. She was shaken, but the incident seemed relatively insignificant at the time. As the weeks went on, however, her health went into a steep decline. She was diagnosed in the fall of 1926 as having inoperable cancer.

On January 2, 1927, she died at her home in Chicago. Her fiance, Ed Sullivan, sat at her bedside and held her hand.

Sybil was elected to the Swimming Hall of Fame in 1967. That organization's museum in Ft. Lauderdale asked Sullivan to do a recording to accompany her picture on the Swim Hall's "Wall of Honor."

He did so, and this is what he said:

"In the days of the great Johnny Weissmuller, Duke Kahanamoku, Gertrude Ederle, and Buster Crabbe, Northwestern University's Sybil Bauer won the Olympic 100-meter backstroke in 1922 and 1923. In 1924 and 1925, Sybil won the Olympic 200-meter backstroke. In 1921, '22, '23, '24, '25, and '26, Sybil won the Olympic 100-yard backstroke.

"Sybil, a girl from Chicago, was a very attractive girl. Most of us sports broadcasters had a crush on her. I know I did. Sybil really belongs in the Swimming Hall of Fame."

It is, all in all, a curious statement on Sullivan's part. Cool, impersonal, and riddled with errors of fact. Perhaps the years had diminished the memory of the soap opera romance of his youth. Or perhaps, as one family member so neatly puts it, "he only agreed to marry her in the first place because he knew she was dying."

There is no question Sylvia Weinstein was, or grew to be, the great love of Sullivan's life. Despite occasional forays into the netherland of chorus girls and actresses, she remained so throughout their life together.

They met at a nightclub called the Casa Lopez in New York where the strolling violinist was a young musician named Xavier Cugat. Sullivan went there frequently but it was Sylvia's first visit. He saw her at the next table and asked Joe Russell, publicity man for the club, to introduce him.

Sylvia was the daughter of Julius Weinstein, a New York real estate man who was to lose most of his money in the Depression. She sometimes described her background as "the regular Marjorie Morningstar world of the time."

It was to be, for the next three and a half years, a stormy, on again, off again, kind of romance.

There was, of course, the religious difference. Ed was Catholic; Sylvia was Jewish. Most published accounts of their relationship—including some by Sullivan himself—say this did not cause any family problems. This is not true. Sullivan's family was extremely opposed to the marriage and in fact, after the wedding it was to be several years (and then only at Sylvia's urging) before the rest of his family began speaking to Ed again.

In April 1930, Ed finally and somewhat reluctantly agreed to get married. Not before he had extracted a promise, however. His children, if any, would be raised Catholic.

The wedding was supposed to be a secret. They met at City Hall and the witnesses were Sylvia's friend, Ruth Sanburg, and Ed's friends, Jim Kahn and Johnny Dundee. They were assured that the marriage would not be made public until Ed gave the word. This would be after the Roman Catholic wedding service was performed the next day. They would then spend a two-day honeymoon in Atlantic City. Then they would tell their parents.

Some enterprising reporters found out that day, however, and Ed and Sylvia had to tell their respective families before they read about the event in the newspapers. Sylvia's family took the news well; Ed's did not.

The date was April 28, 1930. On December 22 of that year, their first and only child, Elizabeth, was born.

For Betty Sullivan it was never to be a normal family life. Her father and mother were both products of that peculiar Victorian attitude that children were better seen and not heard, at least until they were old enough to have something to say. Their primary allegiance was to each other and it remained that way throughout their lives.

So complete was Sylvia's devotion to Ed that after he once mentioned he didn't like lipstick, Sylvia refused to wear it for years.

Although he mellowed a little over the years, Sullivan's attitudes toward women remained somewhat Victorian. Quite simply, he disliked and mistrusted strong-willed independent women. The longevity of his marriage to Sylvia was a testimony to her somewhat passive nature.

For example, one day in May 1933 Sullivan saw Marlene Dietrich at a Broadway show and didn't like the way she was dressed. She was wearing slacks. He rushed to his typewriter and wrote:

"Marlene Dietrich showed plenty of 'ham' by appearing in

92

men's clothes at the Saturday matinee of 'Take a Chance.' She sat in Row A, talked loudly and then got up in the middle of the Haley-Merman number and walked out. . . . Well, what can you expect from one of Hitler's cuties?"

A couple of years later he attacked Joan Crawford after she refused to appear in a charity ball he was hosting.

"One wonders how Joan Crawford has gotten this far in show business with so little talent," he wrote. "No longer will this pillar rush to her defense when other movie stars put the blast on her for her insincerity, or for her affectations."

Kate Smith received this salutation: "When she was on the way up, song publishers were unanimously behind her. Today the same Smith woman is cordially disliked because of her attempt to ritz the crowd who started her off. She even insists that they now address her as Miss Smith."

Joan Crawford got her revenge, though. She sent an open letter to a fan magazine charging that Sullivan's attempt to force her into "a newspaper publicity stunt" was "cheap, tawdry, and gangster journalism." She allowed that she couldn't understand respectable newspapers that "permit journalistic lice to stink up their pages."

Years later, Sullivan ran up against another tough lady named Mary Tyler Moore. She had been signed for two appearances on the show at $7,500 an appearance. Sullivan thought she was going to sing live, but Moore insisted that her song be prerecorded and she mouth the lyrics. There was yelling and screaming and Mary was off the program. She went to court and collected $7,500 for her trouble.

Ironically, Sullivan's daughter, Betty, was to grow up to be a strong and independent woman. It could hardly have been predicted in the beginning, though.

Betty's early life was a succession of paid companions, free movie passes, and lonely dinners at Child's. Ed and Sylvia ate dinner out together, as they did for most of their lives. It was only when Betty turned twelve that she was invited to come along.

"I had a choice," says Betty, now Mrs. Robert Precht and the mother of five. "I could grow up neurotic or I could adjust to the idea that they loved each other first and me second. Looking back, though, I really can't say they were wrong. It was the right lifestyle for them."

His Broadway columns were widely read in those days, but the young and ambitious Sullivan was always looking for a new hustle, a way to make extra money and gain further recognition. There was a short-lived radio program in 1930, which Walter Winchell would later claim he arranged for Sullivan. It is remembered primarily because on March 29 of that year it introduced a young comic named Jack Benny to radio. Benny, of course, went on to become radio's biggest star, but Sullivan watched his show get cancelled after a few weeks. Although he also introduced a number of other notables to the new medium—George M. Cohan, Flo Ziegfeld, Jimmy Durante, Gertrude Nielsen, Jack Haley, Frances Langford, and Irving Berlin, to name a few—he never became a popular radio performer in the manner of Winchell.

There was also in 1932 a disastrous venture into filmmaking, entitled *Mr. Broadway*. Walter Lang, a well-known cameraman for Cecil B. DeMille, owned a large optical house in New York and Sullivan was able to convince Lang and a film laboratory to back the movie. Sullivan wrote and starred in the picture, which is so obscure it isn't listed in the comprehensive *New York Times Review of Films*. Interviewed in a book called *King of the Bs*, the director, Edgar G. Ulmer, said he "didn't like it at all, because Sullivan forced it into one of these moonlight-and-pretzel things. It was a nightmare, a mixture of all kinds of styles."

Sullivan's most successful money-making venture turned out to be vaudeville. Legend has it that he was approached by the manager of the Paramount Theater about doing a show at $1,500 a week for a two-week stint. "You're crazy," Sullivan supposedly said. The manager, thinking Sullivan was negotiating, raised the ante to $3,000 a week. Like many stories

Sullivan enjoyed telling in his later years, this one may or may not be true. There can be little doubt, though, that Sullivan let it be known that his services were available.

Vaudeville was a grinding business—five shows a day, each lasting about an hour. It was not an easy way to make a buck, but it was lucrative and Sullivan enjoyed appearing before a live audience.

From 1932 right up until the birth of *Toast of the Town* in 1948, Sullivan made annual appearances on vaudeville stages in New York and even took touring companies across the country. In short, he was not quite the amateur performer that many people assumed when he burst into fame on the home screen.

A review of one of Sullivan's early vaudeville efforts is instructive because, with the names of the performers changed, it might just as well be a review of one of his television shows thirty years later:

"Ed Sullivan, Broadway columnist, with his third edition of the *Dawn Patrol Revue,* consisting of six night club acts, is on stage this week at Loew's State Theatre. In his third appearance here, Mr. Sullivan is much more at ease than he was in his debut, doing a commendable job as master of ceremonies. The highlight of his own contribution to the entertainment is the showing of motion pictures of former film stars and Broadway figures, during which Mr. Sullivan is narrator.

"The current six acts are novel to State patrons because they are not stock vaudeville interludes. Gross and Dunn, billed as 'song stylists,' are in the featured spot, offering songs in a manner reminiscent of the famous Van and Schenck. Dave Vine, one of the most observant of Jewish dialect comics, carries the heavy comedy burden nicely, delivering plenty of laughs. Babs Ryan and Her Brothers, harmony singers, offer a pleasantly novel song style. Peg Leg Bates, a one-legged Negro tap and acrobatic dancer, proved a sensation at yesterday's matinee with his amazingly facile routines. Rita Rio, singer, opens the show in the accepted hot-cha fashion. Ruby Zwerling and State Senators are on stage this week as part of the unit.

"The motion picture presentation is *Broadway Gondolier*, co-starring Joan Blondell and Dick Powell."

That was 1935. Compare the review to this one from 1955:

"Ed Sullivan had a diversified entertainment layout on his CBS-TV hour Sunday night. Standout on the show were two novelty acts, both involving spectacular body maneuvering.

"One, the Morlidor Trio, had a 23-year-old German making like an India rubber man with an assist from two sturdy gals. In the other, the femme member of the dance team of Holger and Dolores combined lithesome footwork with astounding acro bits of the split and balancing variety.

"The Four Aces, in the opening slot, switched from their usual straight songstering to a jazzed-up 'Saints Go Marching In.' Tony Martin, piped in from Boston, registered pleasantly on two tunes, while vocalists Barbara McNair and LuAnn Simms were okay in individual offerings.

"Joe E. Lewis was spotted briefly for a few laughs. Ventro Ricky Lane and his dummy Velvel, also scored in the humor department, as did the pint-size Tun Tun with his frenetic movement in an imitation of Elvis Presley and in a terp bit with the Dunhills, a neat tap trio.

"Les Garcons de la Rue weren't too impressive in their comedy-songstering contribution. The West Point Glee Club showed up impressively."

In 1936, Sullivan began hosting a vaudeville show featuring the winners of the *Daily News'* annual Harvest Moon Ball, a dance contest sponsored by that newspaper. Each year, for two weeks, the amateur dancers would be given a chance to show their stuff onstage at Loew's State. The event became so popular that Loew's frequently had to add an extra show each day. In 1938, for example, the theater took in $30,000 each of the two weeks. This is even more impressive when you realize that the top nighttime admission was seventy-five cents, afternoon admission was thirty-five cents, and if you got there before noon it was twenty-five cents.

It was here at Loew's State that Sullivan met Carmine

Santullo, then a skinny young cobbler's son from the Bronx, who was to become his faithful servant and man-Friday in the years ahead. Sullivan would write his column backstage at Loew's State and Carmine, who worked there as a bootblack, would run it over to the *Daily News* building.

Though he was now a family man, Sullivan never lost his eye for the ladies, as the following excerpt from a 1934 column shows:

"Where do they come from? . . . 'They,' in this particular instance, being the gorgeous youngsters who decorate the chorus lines of Broadway nite clubs and musical shows. . . . To solve the problem of supply, I've just completed a survey of 241 chorines and showgirls now working on the Stem. . . . For the purpose of statistical information, I studied the decorative personnel of the Ziegfeld 'Follies,' 'White Horse Inn,' Radio City Rockettes, the Gae Foster girls at the Roxy, 'New Faces' and the three big white cabaret shows, Paradise, Ben Marden's Riviera and the Hollywood. . . ." The results of Sullivan's survey are not very interesting, but his research must have been fascinating. Throughout his life Sullivan maintained his interest in a shapely leg and production people from the television show recall that he practically had to be handcuffed whenever Juliet Prowse was on.

Even the showgirls, however, could not blind Sullivan to the fact that the entertainment capital of America was moving West. In 1936 he began making his pitch for a transfer to California and the move was finally slated.

There were compelling reasons why the *News'* top gossip columnist should be in Hollywood, not the least of which was the fact that Tinseltown was where all the good dirt was being created. Louella Parsons was serving up a delicious cup of daily venom for the rival Hearst organization. Winchell's "On Broadway" often originated from Hollywood.

Captain Patterson was willing to send Sullivan to the Coast, but there was one obstacle. Sidney Skolsky had been writing a Hollywood column for the *News* for four years and he liked it.

Skolsky knew what Sullivan had also figured out; that having an influential column originating from the movie colony brought with it a number of fringe benefits.

The Hollywood studio powers had discovered an interesting truth: newspapermen might not be easily bought, but they could be rented. It didn't hurt to have gossip columnists working for you, rather than against you.

Consider these film examples: *Broadway Thru a Keyhole*, 1933, Walter Winchell, original author. Winchell also appeared as an actor in *Wake Up and Live*, 1937, and *Love and Kisses*, 1938. *Hotel for Women*, 1938, Elsa Maxwell, original author and actress. She also appeared in *Public Deb. No. 1*, 1940, and *Stage Door Canteen*, 1943. *Hollywood Hotel*, 1938, based on Louella Parsons's highly successful radio program of the same name and featuring an appearance by the dear one herself. Not to mention *The Daring Young Man*, 1935, based on a story by Sidney Skolsky.

Small wonder, then, that Sullivan was feeling a bit left out. He persisted in his campaign and finally convinced his editors that Skolsky was entirely too chummy with the people he was supposed to be writing about. The *News* ordered Skolsky to swap places with Sullivan. He promptly resigned and issued a statement:

> The *News* assigned me to Hollywood for a year to do a column. I have been here four years. The *News* wanted me to return to do a Broadway column. I believe that Broadway columns are as passé as Broadway. Therefore, I have resigned. They got me wrong. I love Hollywood.

With Skolsky out of the way, the Sullivans—Ed, Sylvia and six-year-old Betty—packed and in September 1937 moved to the Coast. Naturally, they moved into a house in Beverly Hills. It was to be the only period of their marriage when they lived in a house, rather than a hotel.

Sullivan's fling with the movies was to turn out even more

disastrously than his attempts in radio. He wound up with three "based on an original story by" credits and appeared in one of these during his three years in Hollywood. The first of these—*Ma! He's Making Eyes at Me*—was released in late April 1937 and got a cruel reception. *The New York Times* described it as ". . . a cut-rate, bargain basement story about a press agent who builds up a beautiful model as Miss Manhattan in order to sell a cheap line of goods, arranges a stunt marriage for her, and then marries her himself." The *Times* went on to call it "a limp and foolish little picture, inexcusable on any other grounds than as a chaser to follow the main feature." The picture starred Tom Brown and Constance Moore (who sang the title song which was quite popular at the time and which, apparently, had no relationship whatsoever to the plot).

Sullivan's second credit—*There Goes My Heart,* released in October 1938—was even more embarrassing in many ways. It had a fine cast which included Frederic March, Virginia Bruce, and Patsy Kelly and it wasn't badly done. The only problem was that the plot was a direct steal from *It Happened One Night,* the classic Clark Gable-Claudette Colbert film of four years earlier. The "based on an original story by Ed Sullivan" credit had most of Hollywood snickering up its collective sleeve. Said one critic: "Give Sullivan credit· he knows a good comedy when he sees one, which is the next best thing to knowing a good comedy when you write one."

Finally, there was *Big Town Czar,* released in May 1939, in which Sullivan made his acting debut with Barton MacLane, Tom Brown, and Eve Arden. Universal made a real effort to make this one work. A handful of publicity pictures survive showing Sullivan, dressed to the teeth and trying his damnedest to look like Cary Grant, but alas, the critics were again unkind.

Frank S. Nugent of the *Times* wrote: "A bustling little melodrama, all puffed up with its own unimportance, is *Big Town Czar,* which the Criterion presented yesterday. It was written by Ed Sullivan in his best water-under-the-bridge style, which, as you know, is extremely first-personal, quite sentimental, and edifyingly moralistic. His subject is a self-made gangster who realizes too late—on the threshold of the death chamber, in fact—that crime doesn't pay. The gang lord's kid brother has been drawn into the racket and killed, his poor old father and mother are heart-broken, the girl who once loved him has turned sadly away. Only Ed Sullivan, columnist and Greek chorus of the film, remains to pen his memoirs and append the moral to his tale."

Then, the unkindest cut of all, Nugent wrote: ". . . the only word for Ed Sullivan's portrayal of Ed Sullivan is 'unconvincing.'"

Sullivan was later able to look back on these days with a sense of humor but at the time, 1939, it was obvious to everyone, including himself, that he was finished as an actor or screenwriter.

When he was signed to play himself in *Bye, Bye Birdie* in 1962, Sullivan gave an interview to UPI in which he remembered his early days in Hollywood.

"I think the first time I was in a picture was when I came out here in 1937," he said. "I wrote the story and narrated the opening of it. It set Hollywood back 30 years. That was the start of Hollywood's downfall. It's been going downhill ever since." He went on to say: "There's something suspicious about my acting career. Nobody has ever asked me back. I'm getting very sensitive about it. I can take a hint as well as the next guy."

By this time, of course, Sullivan could afford to be jocular about his career. Television had made him the star he had always wanted to be, a kind of deity, as was suggested by that wonderful moment in *Bye, Bye Birdie* when Paul Lynde and family, dressed in choir robes, sing a hymn to him:

> Ed Sullivan. Ed Sullivan.
> We're going to be on Ed Sullivan.
> We'll be coast to coast
> With our favorite host,
> Ed Sull-i-van.

Sullivan was, it might be noted, fairly convincing as himself in *Birdie* and further developed the role in Jerry Lewis's *The Patsy* in 1964 and *The Singing Nun* in 1965. Sullivan had played a major role in bringing Sister Anne, the Dominican nun whose recording of "Dominique" had captured the world's fancy, to the American public. The film recreated his flight to Belgium, arrival at Fichermont Convent and his petition to its Mother Superior to film and record Sister Anne's music.

But in 1940 Sullivan had no reason to suspect that he would ever appear in a picture again, much less have his life story considered worthy of film immortalization. He was washed up in the film colony and he knew it. Once again, fame had eluded him. Rumors began appearing in the trade papers that he and John Chapman of the *Daily News* were about to swap positions.

Sullivan's sisters, Helen and Frances, took the train out to California to visit in the summer of 1940. They found Ed moody and distracted. He still had a great deal of influence in the movie capital. Groucho Marx invited them to dinner. Edward G. Robinson showed them his collection of impressionist paintings and Walt Disney gave them a tour. But something was clearly amiss. After a few days, Helen and Frances took off on their own to visit Yosemite. Ed was disappointed and hurt.

It is speculation, of course, but Sullivan may have had additional pressures—more than simply his failing career in the movies. He had developed an inordinate fondness for horse racing and was losing big at Hollywood Park and Santa Anita. The house they lived in at 621 North Alta was modest enough, had once belonged to Larry Hart, but there were Betty's private companions and school.

So it is likely that Sullivan had financial problems during this period. In any event, Sullivan knew he had to get out of Hollywood and fast. Around Christmas 1940, the Sullivans returned to Broadway.

Saddest to leave was ten-year-old Betty. For her, California had meant freedom, a chance to live like a normal child in a real house with a real backyard. Being the daughter of a famous columnist meant things like answering the door and finding cowboy star Gene Autry standing there. It meant being invited to Shirley Temple's birthday parties.

In short, it was a magical time. She decided there and then that she would return someday. As a teen-ager, she often visited California in the summers and stayed with her friend, Barbara Whiting. There was never really any doubt that she would attend UCLA after she finished high school. California was a happy place for her.

This rare photograph was taken on the morning of June 20, 1948, during rehearsal for *Toast of the Town*'s premiere that evening. Sullivan is at center, flanked on the left by Richard Rodgers and on the right by Oscar Hammerstein III. Readers will easily recognize Dean Martin (that's Monica Lewis whispering in his ear) and Jerry Lewis. To the left of Lewis is James Kirkwood, whose act (with partner Lee Goodman) was cut before the broadcast. (CBS)

Above: The always polite Elvis Presley posed for this publicity shot at the request of Brazilian singer Leny Eversong, the charmingly large lady in the center. (Wide World) Below: A Moiseyev dancer is captured in mid-flight. This great Russian dance troupe provided one of Sullivan's finest cultural hours.

Above: Ed and his wife Sylvia in Tel-Aviv with Israeli premier David Ben-Gurion on August 31, 1958. (Wide World)   Below: Sullivan, flanked by his two favorite ladies: daughter, Betty (left) and wife, Sylvia (right). The photo was taken upon their departure for Europe and Israel in 1958. (Wide World)   Right: One of Sullivan's "discoveries" on his 1958 visit to Israel was 12-year-old violinist Itzhak Perlman. Young Perlman first appeared on the show on February 11, 1958. (Wide World)

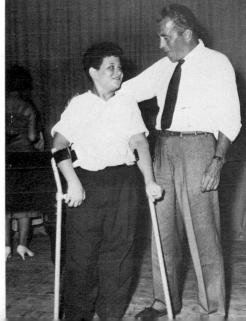

Sullivan in animated conversation with Fidel Castro on the eve of the bearded Cuban's triumphant march into Havana. The interview—Sullivan's finest journalistic scoop—was arranged by Chicago Tribune correspondent Jules Dubois (the gringo in the white suit beside Castro). (Manny Alpert)

Above: Ed and his little Italian puppet friend Topo Gigo. Kiss-a-me goodnight, Eddie. (CBS) Below: Ed joins a party of super groups in London in April 1964. Recognizable in the photograph are the late Brian Epstein, George Harrison, Peter, Paul, and Mary, and John Lennon. That's the back of Ringo's head and Paul McCartney's ear and sideburns. (Wide World)

Ed makes up with Jackie Mason following their celebrated feud. After this appearance in 1966, Mason was never invited back. (Wide World)

Sullivan and son-in-law Bob Precht share a laugh with stage manager Ed Brinkman. (Wide World)

Ed hams it up in a comedy skit with Johnny Wayne (l.) and Frank Shuster. Wayne & Shuster appeared on the show 67 times. (CBC)

The great impersonators doing their Sullivan bits. Will Jordan (left) was first and, in many opinions, best; Jack Carter was just okay, but John Byner seemed able, in Bob Precht's words "to get right inside Ed's head." (CBS)

Above: Sullivan played Sullivan in the 1968 MGM movie *The Singing Nun*. The other principals are, from left, Greer Garson, Ricardo Montalban, Agnes Moorehead, and Debbie Reynolds. (Wide World)   Below: Ed and old friend Carmine Santullo in a photograph taken shortly before Sullivan's death in 1973. (Sullivan Productions)

The War and After

The war years were difficult for Sullivan. He was thirty-eight at the time of Pearl Harbor, too old to be drafted, and the army wouldn't have taken him because of his ulcer, anyway. He was in great pain most of the time and could eat only the mildest of foods.

After their return from Hollywood, the Sullivans moved into a small suite at the Astor Hotel. There was no refrigerator and Betty recalls hearing him get up often in the middle of the night to get a drink of milk from a carton he kept on the window sill in winter.

Sullivan threw himself into a breakneck schedule of benefits and charity drives. In 1942, he staged a massive show for Army Emergency Relief and grossed $226,500. A year later, at Madison Square Garden, he staged a second and even bigger show that grossed $249,000. He organized performing troupes for hospitals and troop camps. He was determined, it seems, to prove that he was doing his share for the war effort.

Through it all, in his column, he allowed no good deed of his own to go unreported. His writing during that period was sentimental and frequently tearjerking. Tales of the courage of one-armed and dying soldiers filled his musings daily. Unlike Damon Runyon, who used sentimentality in a cynical and opportunistic way, Sullivan really was a romantic. He really believed what he was writing, even when the facts themselves were distorted. Unfortunately, hc lacked Runyon's skill and many of the stories he wrote were more morbid than touching.

So pronounced was Sullivan's penchant for self-flattery that his column became something of a joke to other newspapermen. Harriet Van Horne, then a young reporter on the *World-Telegram,* wrote a hilarious takeoff on a Sullivan column and put it on the newspaper's bulletin board. The city editor thought it was funny, too, and ran it in the newspaper.

Sullivan was incensed. He sent Miss Van Horne a scathing letter and he never forgave her. Years later, after she had written some relatively minor criticism of the TV show, he sent her a wire that read: "Dear Miss Van Horne. You Bitch. Sincerely, Ed Sullivan."

Sullivan tried his hand at producing in early 1941 when he attempted to rescue a show called *Crazy with the Heat,* that had expired after only seven nights on Broadway. The show, more a series of vignettes and vaudeville-style interludes, had gone through a series of re-writes and out-of-town performances before it arrived—still half-baked—on the Great White Way. Interesting, in a footnote sort of way, is the fact that Milton Berle wrote some of the sketches that were dropped before the show opened in New York. Producer Kurt Kasznar and his backers were out $165,000.

Sullivan somehow managed to raise $20,000 to re-open the show after it had been closed for twelve days. During that time, he had almost completely revised it. Willie Howard and Luella Gear were still the stars, but he had dropped some of the acts and added new ones. Specifically, he had gone through the reviews of the first production and eliminated everything to which the critics had objected.

This experiment in creative democracy still did not please the critics, however, and after ninety-two performances the show closed again. Never one to give up on something, Sullivan later revised the show a little more and booked it into the Loew's State vaudeville house—where it should have been in the first place—and it enjoyed some success. Another interesting footnote: Victor Borge was in the Sullivan Broadway production, playing the piano—straight—for singer Gracie Barrie.

Sullivan's motives in attempting to rescue what seems to have been an obviously lost cause are not clear. No doubt the vaudeville nature of the show appealed to him. Also, he was having one of his little romantic flings with one of the actresses in the show.

In 1942, Sullivan tried his hand at production again, this time an all-black revue called *Harlem Cavalcade*. Many black performers were out of work at the time and although Sullivan must have known that the odds were against him (there hadn't been a successful black show since Lew Leslie's *Blackbirds of 1928*), several of the singers and dancers had helped him with his Madison Square Garden benefit and he felt indebted. The performers included Noble Sissle and his orchestra, Flourney Miller, Moke and Poke, Pops and Louis, the Peters Sisters, Bob and Wini Johnson, and Jimmie Daniels. From the Apollo Theater he got popular comedians Monte Hawley and Johnny Lee, and the chorus line was recruited largely from the Ubangi Club. The show was received rather well and kept its principals employed for several months.

In 1944, the Sullivans moved from the Astor to the Delmonico Hotel on Park Avenue at 59th Street and they remained there for the rest of their lives. Betty was a teen-ager now, attending Miss Hewlett's School. Many of the kids who went there were rich brats and Betty often felt stigmatized by being the daughter of a "gossip" columnist.

Now that she was a small adult, Sullivan began to take more of an interest in Betty. She was invited to join the family

105

dinners at fancy restaurants like Pavillion or The Colony.

"It was hard spending three hours at dinner and then getting my homework done," she recalls. "And you couldn't just sit there quietly and eat. My father insisted that you take part in discussions and talk. I remember telling mother that I would rather fix myself something at home and she got out a hot plate and was going to teach me to cook. Well, she cooked a couple of meals and they were just disasters. I decided I'd rather take my chances on the restaurants."

The Park Avenue hotel and the fancy restaurants and the private school for Betty were not inexpensive and Sullivan had to hustle more and more to make ends meet. He had his column and his once-a-year vaudeville stint and he still felt he could make a go at radio. CBS gave him another shot in 1945 with a show called *Ed Sullivan Entertains*. The program originated from "21" and featured Sullivan interviewing famous people. *Variety* reviewed it this way:

"*Ed Sullivan Entertains* is the tag of this new 15-minuter which is showmanly spotted in Club 21, as the emanation point, and hence a plausible excuse for the celebrity parade. While it's sponsored by Mennen's, the credits are spread wide, both for New York *News* syndicated columnist Sullivan who emcees; the 21 Club, which gets a good commercial trailer cuffo, because of its general background; plus whatever kudos which automatically falls to the lot of the sundry guests.

"Constance Bennett, wife of Lieutenant Gilbert Roland, was first introed, and there was a play on 'from Gilbert to Sullivan.' Ona Munson was mentioned in passing; there was a salute to Captain Clark Gable; and then Berlin, Pfc. Dana Babcock, and Melville Cooper joined the mikesters. The marine, surprisingly, seemed the most at ease and the least mike-conscious.

"Cooper, featured in *Merry Widow,* set the pace for what will be a regular routine, a casual 'interrupter,' i.e., pseudo-habitué of 21 who just 'happens along.' Actually, of course, the broadcast from the upstairs back room of the famed bistro is roped off for the occasion.

"Berlin had the meatiest session, touching on his song hits, how long it takes to write them, his favorites, etc. He labeled 'Alexander's Ragtime Band' Number 1 generally; 'Hate to Get Up in the Morning' as his top war song; 'Pretty Girl Is Like a Melody' for ballad; and 'White Christmas' which, having sold over 1,000,000 copies, he says may become the most popular of all his tunes. Sullivan asked him about 'God Bless America' and Berlin stated 'that's in a class all by itself.' There were references, naturally, to 'Yip Yip Yaphank' and 'This Is the Army,' all of it solid.

"The commercials were good, with Mennen's new skin dermatology product getting the trailer. A 'late news flash from the New York *Daily Newsroom*' is a good interrupter before the final commercial and also the trailer for next week's guesters. Joe McCarthy of the Yanks was the only one heralded on the debut broadcast.

"Withal, a bright quarter hour having more substance than the usual celebrity interview sessions in that a name emcee, Sullivan, himself no slouch as a conferencier, is at the helm. Coupled with this are the glamour auspices, strong names he's bound to line up, the aura of the 21 setting, and the CBS outlet at a favorable dinner hour on a day—Monday—when most families are home."

That show, too, soon folded and Sullivan once again found himself the loser in his running battle with Walter Winchell, whose radio program continued to rule the airwaves.

Sullivan's mood was often sour in those days. Sometimes he would explode in a fit of temper over some relatively small thing and storm out of the apartment and stay away for hours. Other times, he would brood. Time seemed to be catching up with him. Despite his ulcer, he would sometimes drink.

"He was ambitious and almost totally undisciplined," Betty says. "If he knew he had to do something, it would be the last

107

thing he got around to doing. He could not stand to be constrained in any way. When he wanted to, he could write very well, but he simply couldn't face the idea that he had to do it."

Christmas was the worst time for Sullivan. He absolutely hated holidays. Coupled with Christmas itself, Sylvia's birthday was December 21 and Betty's, December 22. To him, that meant having to do certain things and that, in turn, was a kind of discipline.

Betty was never really sure whether he would bring home a Christmas tree or not because he always put it off until the last moment. Christmas Eve, 1945, he came home carrying a feeble-looking bush that had been painted silver.

"That's not a Christmas tree," Betty said.

"Yes, it is," Sullivan answered.

"It is not," Betty said. "It's ugly and it's not a tree and I don't like it."

"Fine," Sullivan said. "We won't have a tree this year." He took the bush, threw it into the hallway, then stormed into the bedroom and closed the door.

Betty was shattered. She and Sylvia, both in tears, went off to eat dinner at Pavillion without Sullivan, who refused to come out of the bedroom.

Later that evening, Betty—her eyes still red from crying—and her mother returned home. Sitting there, in the middle of the room, was a handsome Christmas tree. For Betty, the lonely child, it was one of the happiest moments of her life.

Mrs. Winchell's Little Boy

One humid summer evening in 1952 the Sullivans went to dinner at the Stork Club with a young assistant from the *Toast of the Town* production staff. Winchell was there, as he usually was, at table 50 in the Cub Room and Sullivan, as he invariably did when he found himself in the same room with Mrs. Winchell's little boy Walter, demanded a table facing his arch enemy. Sullivan seemed to derive a peculiar pleasure from staring Winchell down in public places and never missed an opportunity to do so, although it made his ulcer hurt and left Sylvia a nervous wreck.

Things were different these days. For the first time in their thirty-year rivalry, Sullivan clearly had the upper hand. Television had brought him the recognition that he had never achieved with his column or in vaudeville and radio. Winchell was rapidly becoming irrelevant. People didn't much care what Broadway or movie stars were doing or who they were doing it with. The public was busy discovering credit cards and lawn sprinklers. Those glamorous, remote personalities now came into everybody's home at night via the little talking box in the living room. Gossip was at a low ebb.

It had not always been so. Walter Winchell had been, since 1925, one of the most powerful men in America. At his peak, his column was syndicated in nearly 1,000 newspapers. His radio broadcasts—launched in his staccato style of delivery with "Good evening, Mr. and Mrs. America and all the ships at sea. Let's go to press"—were listened to by an estimated one third of the adult population. On at least one occasion he found himself in the embarrassing position of being shadowed by bodyguards supplied by his pal, J. Edgar Hoover, *and* by his equally good friend, Lucky Luciano.

Winchell was undisputedly the father of modern gutter journalism. He could make a bestseller out of a piece of trash that he had never even read by mentioning it in his column. And did. He could ruin an actor's career by accusing him, usually falsely, of being a homosexual or a communist. And did. He could get the prettiest girls on Broadway into his bed with promises of mentions in his column. And he didn't even always keep his promise. He spawned dozens of imitators, including Ed Sullivan, but none of them were ever able to capture his raspy, abrasive, and compulsively readable style. Even when his stuff was pure fantasy—and it often was—it was compelling.

The war between these two middle-aged bulldogs, staring at each other across a nightclub floor, began in 1929 when Sullivan was a young sportswriter for the *Graphic* and Winchell was its star columnist. It had continued unabated for these many years.

More than any petty slight, or series of them, the thing that must have annoyed Sullivan most over the years was the fact that he was always cast as a Winchell imitator. Winchell invented modern gossip journalism; Sullivan inherited his column and style. Winchell had a successful radio show; Sullivan got a radio show that was not. Winchell hosted vaudeville shows; Sullivan began hosting vaudeville shows.

Until his enormous success in television, Sullivan had lived in Winchell's shadow.

"No wonder I was always tense and moody," Sullivan once admitted to his colleague, Robert Sylvester. "I would have a radio show, have it get cancelled, then I would turn on my set on Sunday night and there he was. That staccato voice calling to 'Mr. and Mrs. America and all the ships at sea' and me realizing that America was listening. I didn't even have the comfort of telling myself that he was lousy. He wasn't good. He was simply great. I would grow another small ulcer and start planning another radio show. I'd get it on. And somebody would quickly get it off."

And the fact of the matter is, Sullivan was never in Winchell's league as a gossip columnist. He quite simply lacked WW's instinct for the jugular. Winchell was, as John Crosby observed after his death, "a 14-carat sonofabitch." Sullivan could be on occasion but it was not his true nature.

Despite his personal disdain for Winchell, Sullivan had a grudging respect for what his rival's ruthlessness had accomplished. They also had more in common than was widely known by the general public.

Winchell was fairly open about his affairs with women, often referring to mysterious "baby dolls" and chorus girls in his column and, as frequently as not, even mentioning them by name. Sullivan, on the other hand, was a discreet player. Perhaps it was Catholic guilt or maybe just good taste but he never had the urge to go public with his encounters. They shared similar appetites, however, girls with long legs and nice bottoms. Neither was particularly interested in large chests. They had at least two, and possibly more, dalliances in common; one, a beautiful dancer who was once part of a sister act, and another brunette singer with great legs who had had a major supporting role in a Broadway musical.

And as with everything else, except television, Winchell had been first there, too.

Over the years, the Winchell-Sullivan feud had remained a

rather private one and its intensity was known mainly to intimates and show business insiders. The *Daily News* had a policy of editing Winchell's name out of Sullivan's column on the grounds that it was simply free advertising for the rival columnist. Perhaps, too, as the previous paragraphs suggest, neither man wanted to really open up with everything he knew about the other.

On this particular night at the Stork Club, Sullivan was especially incensed at Winchell. A few weeks earlier, the black American star of the Folies Bergere, Josephine Baker, had gone to the Stork Club with a friend. She sat for an hour while staff and management pretended not to notice that she was there. Winchell witnessed this whole sorry affair without comment. Ms. Baker went to Barry Gray, the New York broadcaster, and asked to come on his radio show to tell the story of the incident. Gray allowed her to do so, a decision that was to make his life a living hell for the next three years.

Winchell was outraged at Ms. Baker's comments about him. He denied having been there. He wrote that the black singer was a "traitor to America," that she had sold out to the Nazis when France was occupied by the Wehrmacht and that she was anti-Semitic. Ms. Baker returned to Gray's show, displayed the medal given her by De Gaulle in recognition of her work with the French resistance forces, pointed out that she lived in Paris because she could make a living there, and claimed that she was not anti-Semitic because her husband happened to be Jewish.

Sullivan called Gray and asked if he could come on the show to say a few words in defense of Ms. Baker. Gray was delighted, of course, because most people in show business were laying low at this point, fearing Winchell's wrath. Sullivan came on Gray's show twice and spoke eloquently about human rights.

There had been a Friars Club roast in Hollywood earlier in the summer and, as featured speaker, Winchell had taken the opportunity to castigate his fellow New York columnists, most particularly Sullivan and a former protege, Leonard Lyons.

Sullivan had responded in his usual Saturday column, "My Secretary, Africa, Speaks" (patterned, alas, after Winchell's "Girl Friday" column) by writing: "Jack Benny, George Burns, George Jessel, and other Coast performers who belong to the L.A. lodge of the Friars applied their own yardstick to Hollywood hokum this week. They permitted a visiting newspaperman to acknowledge the dinner in his honor by blasting other New York newspapermen. In New York, if such a bizarre, tactless thing had happened, Friars at the head table would immediately have disassociated the club from the guest's slander of newspapermen, who have been pretty good friends of performers. Apparently, this didn't occur to Abbot Benny. Lyrical intro of the guest was delivered by Jessel. At the ASCAP dinner in New York recently, Jessel bored locals at the head table with his off-the-record emphasis that the guy he later eulogized at the Friars' Coast party was a complete no-good."

There was one other factor that made this particular glaring match more volatile than usual. The young production assistant with the Sullivans had worked for Winchell for a year; "The most miserable year of my life," he now recalls. "Winchell was a truly evil man." Sullivan liked this kid and was aware of the torture he had undergone at Winchell's hands.

Toward the end of the evening, Winchell got up to go to the bathroom. Sullivan immediately put down his glass, wiped his lips on the napkin, said, "Excuse me," and left to follow. Sylvia was distraught. She, like everyone else in the city, was aware that Winchell normally carried a revolver in his pocket. "Follow him," she said, to the young assistant. "Something's going to happen."

The assistant opened the outer door of the restroom gently and stepped inside. There was another inner door and he opened it slightly and peeped inside. What he saw was an extraordinary sight. Ed Sullivan, the king of Sunday night television, was holding the head of Broadway's most influential columnist firmly in the bottom of a urinal and gleefully

113

pumping the flush lever. Winchell was making noises which sounded like sobbing.

"I didn't do anything," the assistant says. "I just turned and quietly walked out."

Oddly enough, this violent episode was the beginning of the end of Sullivan's hatred for Winchell. Like the good kid who has beaten the town bully, Sullivan began to lose his appetite for the battle. Clearly, Winchell was finished anyway.

The *Mirror* folded in 1963 and Winchell watched his empire shrink to fewer than 100 papers who carried his now mellower columns. On Christmas Day, 1968, his son, Walter, Jr., then thirty-three years old, got up from the Christmas dinner table and told his wife and two children that he was going for a walk. He went instead to the garage where he placed a 38-caliber automatic in his mouth and blew the top of his head off. He had been working as a dishwasher and his children were getting welfare payments. Winchell never wrote another line after that.

Two years later, his wife, June, died in Phoenix of a long-standing respiratory ailment. Winchell was a friendless and broken man.

He died of cancer in February 1972 in the UCLA Medical Center at the age of seventy-four. He was buried in Phoenix near the graves of his wife and son. Only his daughter, Walda, and three newspapermen who had been assigned to cover the final chapter, were there for the simple, ten-minute ceremony. "Technically, he died of cancer," Walda said, "but actually of a broken heart." He left behind a fortune of more than $2 million.

There was one large incongruity in Winchell's lifetime of malice toward almost everybody and perhaps it explains Sullivan's willingness to forgive. It was the Damon Runyon Cancer Fund.

During the period when Damon Runyon was dying from throat cancer, he and Winchell became inseparable pals. The New York City police had given Winchell his own police radio and siren and the two big-town turks would go roaring through the streets in search of homicides and other interesting tales of Manhattan. Runyon was the perfect companion for Winchell. For one thing, he was—according to most accounts—almost as big a bastard as his friend and for another his vocal cords had been cut in a futile attempt to halt the cancer. Winchell could never stand to be interrupted and never mastered the art of talking to one person at a time. If he said something particularly outrageous, Runyon would scribble "bullshit" or some equally appropriate epithet on a pad of paper he carried and hand it to Winchell.

After Runyon's death, Winchell established the Damon Runyon Cancer Fund and during his lifetime it raised $37 million for cancer research. Not a penny went for administrative costs. Winchell, a notoriously cheap man who never owned more than eight suits in his life, paid all the costs of running the Fund out of his own pocket. Sullivan took over the Fund after Winchell's death and changed its name to the Damon Runyon-Walter Winchell Cancer Fund. He served as its president until, like the men for whom it was named, he too succumbed to cancer.

Part III

The Ed Sullivan Show: 1955–1971

The Ed Sullivan Show
1955

By 1955, Ed Sullivan was riding high. *Toast of the Town* was consistently in the top ten rated shows, attracting some forty-four million viewers a week. Often as not, it ranked right behind *I Love Lucy* and *The Jackie Gleason Show* as number one in the nation's favor. CBS displayed its gratitude by raising Sullivan's salary to $4,000 a week, giving him a twenty-year no-option contract, and agreeing to rename the show *The Ed Sullivan Show*. Old stone face had arrived.

Several months before his contract was renegotiated, Sullivan let it leak, ever so casually, that "people" at NBC had been talking to him about a defection. Having failed to knock him off with any of their own entries, the story went, they were prepared to try to lure him over. Just how serious these talks were only Sullivan knew and he wasn't saying. In any event, it got him the concessions he wanted from CBS.

As it happened, NBC had a plan of its own. They would throw Steve Allen, a bright young performer who was developing a big following on their late night *Tonight Show*, up against

Sullivan. The new Allen show debuted on June 24, 1955.

The rivalry started off friendly enough. Before his first show, Allen wired Sullivan: "Dear Ed. Would you lend me ten Trendex points till payday? Love and kisses, Steve Allen."

Sullivan thought that was funny and mentioned it in an article he had written for *Collier's.* Discounting stories of a possible feud, Sullivan wrote, "Actually, we are the best of friends."

Allen invited Sullivan to come over to the *Tonight Show* some night for a chat and Sullivan was willing, but CBS shot the proposed appearance down.

During his first month on the air, Allen pulled a coup by lining up Elvis Presley for an appearance. Presley was the hottest performer in the country at the time and Allen got him for the bargain basement price of $5,500. Actually, Elvis had already been on national television a couple of times before— once with Tommy and Jimmy Dorsey and another time on Milton Berle's program.

The Monday after Presley's appearance on the Allen show, Sullivan—as he always did on Mondays—picked up his phone and called a lady named Mary Smith at the Trendex ratings service. "Presley done you in," Mary Smith said. "He racked up 20.2. You had 14.8."

It was a rare defeat for Sullivan and he wasn't pleased. He was particularly mad at himself because some months earlier he had had a chance to sign Elvis for $5,000. He had laughed at the time. Five thousand for some long-haired rock 'n' roller.

Like most adults at the time, Sullivan did not much care for this rock 'n' roll business. Still, kids seemed to like it and he was not the kind of man who would actively dislike anything of which a significant portion of the populace was in favor. He had hesitated to sign Elvis mainly because his first fling with a rock singer had ended so disastrously.

Several months earlier, Sullivan had allowed himself to be talked into booking Bo Diddley, a pioneering but not very talented rock musician. Sullivan had never actually heard Bo sing but he knew from the record ratings that Bo's song—called "Bo Diddley" after himself—was number one in the country.

When he got to the studio on Sunday, Sullivan was chagrined to find that Bo's big hit consisted of the singer strumming the same chords over and over, jumping up and down, and yelling "Bo Diddley, Bo Diddley."

Sullivan wanted to drop the act on the spot but an aide pointed out that they had promised the Diddley appearance the week before and besides there was nobody else around to fill in.

Sullivan wandered over to the orchestra area and picked up the sheet music to "Some Enchanted Evening" and handed it to Diddley. "Sing this," he said.

That night at the telecast, Diddley dutifully began to sing "Some Enchanted Evening." The audience, quite rightfully, began to laugh. They thought it was some sort of gag. Diddley panicked. About sixteen bars into the song, he suddenly started singing his hit, "Bo Diddley." The orchestra—at least until Ray Bloch realized what had happened—continued to play "Some Enchanted Evening." Sullivan was enraged. The whole experience turned him off rock performers and caused him to pass over Elvis.

Now he was sorry. He did the gracious thing, though, and wired Allen: "Steven Presley Allen, NBC-TV, New York City. Stinker. Love and kisses, Ed Sullivan."

A reporter called to get his reaction to Allen's victory. Sullivan allowed that one Sunday did not make a year; that this Presley kid was unsuitable for family viewing, anyway; that he, Sullivan, had better taste than that; that some people would do anything to get good ratings.

Three hours later, from his farm house in Connecticut, Sullivan was on the phone with Colonel Tom Parker, Elvis's manager, negotiating the biggest deal in the history of his show. When the two old lions finished chewing at each other an hour later, Elvis was set for three appearances on the Sullivan show, for a record-breaking $50,000.

Later, he was to explain his change of heart by saying that he

121

had looked at kinescopes of Elvis's appearances on the Dorsey program.

He told TV writer Bob Williams: "I'd been told this guy was disrupting the morals of kids, that his whole appeal was sensual, that he did bumps and grinds and rubbed his thighs when he sang. I saw a guy come on who was a pale replica carbon copy of Johnnie Ray. Johnnie Ray came on our show a few years ago and shouted and got down and beat the floor and frothed at the mouth and every other thing."

Based on what he had seen, he remarked, it was a "frightening, evil thing" what *some* people were saying about Elvis.

And he couldn't resist gloating a bit: "I was shocked to learn that NBC had failed to sign him up for more appearances," he said. "Presley is the hottest thing in television right now. I guarantee we'll have the biggest audience in our eight years of experience when he comes on."

And he was right about that. None of Elvis's previous television appearances had anything like the impact of his first show for Sullivan on September 9. Sullivan, in a masterstroke of showmanship (or, perhaps, a heartfelt sense of propriety) instructed John Wray to shoot Elvis from the waist up only. He also let the nation know what he was doing to protect public morals and somehow hundreds of newspapers around the country found this to be front page copy. So powerful was the force of Sullivan's media hype that even today many people think Elvis made his TV debut on the Sullivan show.

On Elvis's second appearance a few months later—a remote from Hollywood—he was shown discreetly, but more or less full-frontally. The irrepressible Charles Laughton, substituting in New York for Sullivan on that show, introduced the Elvis segment by saying, "Now we go to Hollywood for *Elvin* Presley." So loud were the protests from the New York studio audience that he had to go out on stage and apologize while the segment was still on.

After the Presley incident, Allen and Sullivan clashed frequently. Allen was planning a tribute on his October 14 show to the actor, James Dean, who had recently been killed in an auto crash. He had hardly gotten past the preliminary stages when Sullivan announced that *he* was going to have a Dean tribute on October 14. Not only that, he had lined up Dean's aunt and uncle for a brief appearance and had gotten the rights to show a clip from *Giant,* Dean's last movie.

Allen was furious. He suspected spies in his camp. He had been negotiating with Dean's relatives and also for the rights to the *Giant* clip.

Allen called up the newspapers to protest this "piracy." "I don't believe it's Ed who's making these unethical and cutthroat moves," he said.

He then proceeded to say that it was common knowledge that he had planned the Dean tribute for months and that at the last minute Sullivan had cancelled Vic Damone and Imogene Coca in order to make room for the Dean spot.

Sullivan said Allen was a "cry baby." He added some strange comment about his Dean segment really being a tribute to Edna Ferber, the author of *Giant.* He said it was "ghoulish" how some people were trying to take advantage of the death of that "fine youngster," James Dean.

Vic Damone checked in from Paris to say that he had not been cancelled. He had asked to have his appearance rescheduled for later.

When the dust had settled, Sullivan had the Dean tribute, the film clip, and Dean's aunt and uncle. Not to mention another win in the ratings.

During the height of his troubles with Allen, Sullivan got involved in another controversy, this time with Ingrid Bergman. On July 18, 1956, he announced that the actress, self-exiled from the United States because of her widely publicized romance with Roberto Rossellini, would return that fall and appear on his show. Bergman was in London at the time making *Anastasia,* her first American picture in years. Twentieth Century-Fox made the arrangements, but apparently never asked Bergman.

A week after the Sullivan announcement, Bergman told a London newspaper that there was no truth to the story about an appearance. Sullivan was going to use film excerpts, she said, "but there never was any question of my going to the States with him."

This infuriated Sullivan, who had been made a bit of a fool in public. Meanwhile, he was getting lots of negative mail about Bergman and his sponsor was also upset.

It was in a spirit of anger and pressure that Sullivan took the stage on the July 29 program. He said: "Now the film has been made. Now over there it seemed to me that this thing should be left up to the American audience because you decide everything. I was planning to use the film on our show at some time: she doing a scene with Helen Hayes.

"Now I know that she's a controversial figure, so it's entirely up to you. If you want her on our show, I wish you'd drop me a note and let me know to that effect. And if you don't, if you think it shouldn't be done, you also let me know that too, because I say it's your decision and I'd like to get your verdict on it.

"I think a lot of you know that this woman has had seven and a half years—you know she's had seven and a half years of time for penance. Others may not think so, but whatever you think, it would clarify because everybody's newspaper has called up this morning. When I came into the office they wanted to know what this decision had been on the Ingrid Bergman appearance on our show and I told them what I told you: it's entirely up to the public."

It was Sullivan at his worst, sanctimonious and hypocritical, a total abdication of his responsibility as a producer. The remarks were spur of the moment, made on an impulse that reflected the great pressures he was feeling at the time. They were disgusting even to himself within moments after they

124

were said. As he walked backstage, he turned to talent coordinator Jack Babb and said, "Why the hell did I say that?"

There was, of course, no possibility that Bergman would appear on the show after that. Perhaps there never had been. Sullivan always regretted the incident, though. "Ingrid never forgave me," he admitted a few years later, "and she was right."

Meanwhile, the Allen feud marched on.

Allen had another ratings victory in January 1957 when his guest was Charles Van Doren, a young Columbia University professor who had captured the nation's heart with his incredible victories on the quiz show *Twenty-One*. (A year and a half later, Van Doren would appear before a Senate subcommittee and admit that he had had help with the answers. His confession launched television's most famous scandal.)

Most weeks, though, the Allen show was well behind. Sullivan was never in Allen's league as a performer but as a producer he was far ahead of the Allen camp. Sullivan had a newspaperman's love of the "timely." A guy pitches a no-hitter on Friday; get him for the show on Sunday. Next Sunday is too late. He would bump acts off his show just so he could say, "Here's an act that I caught down in Florida last week when I was vacationing."

A perfect example of a 1957 Sullivan "scoop" involved the arrival at Plymouth Rock of the *Mayflower II*, a historic re-enactment of the original *Mayflower* crossing. Captain Allan Villiers, the vessel's skipper, stepped right off the ship and onto a plane chartered by Sullivan to bring him to the show that night.

Sullivan had signed the captain through the Mayflower Committee several weeks before. Allen's people tried to get him but were, as usual, too late.

The week before this incident, Allen had accused Sullivan of "exploiting" Harry Belafonte's name by promising that Belafonte would be on the Sullivan show and implying that the appearance would be "live." What Sullivan had meant to say was that he would have a clip of Belafonte, who was very hot then, singing in the movie *Island in the Sun*. As it turned out, the CinemaScope film couldn't be adapted to TV and there was no Belafonte. No explanation by Sullivan of why he wasn't there, either.

"We knew he didn't have Belafonte," Allen's manager, Jules Green, says, "because Steve had offered him $25,000 for one show, and he had promised that Steve's would be the first show he went on."

Earl Wilson caught up with Sullivan on the golf course and told him what Allen and Green were saying.

"I have no comment on anything those two punks have to say," Sullivan snapped.

And so it came to pass that Steve Allen went from being a "very good friend" to a "punk" in one year. Later, when Allen was no longer his competitor, Sullivan made peace with him and had him and his wife Jayne Meadows on the show.

After the Belafonte incident, the Sullivan-Allen feud simply died. Sullivan knew Allen was no longer a threat but there was a new competitor on the scene. The nation had gone cowboy crazy and ABC had thrown a new winner called *Maverick* into the Sunday night fray. *Maverick* was to destroy Allen and force the Sullivan show, for the first time, out of the top ten.

Sullivan had another reason to have mellowed. After the accident, he was lucky to be alive.

The Accident

It was well past one o'clock on the morning of August 6, 1956, and Sylvia and Betty were worried. "What's keeping them?" Sylvia wondered, pacing in front of the living room fireplace at the Sullivan country house near Southbury, Connecticut. Ed and Sylvia had bought the 185-acre farm three years before, mainly because they thought it would be a good place to spend some time with son-in-law Bob Precht, who visited on leaves from the Navy, and Betty and their two new grandchildren. Oddly enough, one of the bonuses of the success of the television show was that it had made Sullivan a more conscientious father and grandfather.

Betty, who was lying on the sofa, was worried, too, but she said something about the plane being delayed. She didn't want to alarm her mother. Instead, she stared at an American primitive painting called the "City of Tanjoro" that hung over the fireplace mantel. Try as she might, she could not close out the ticking of the small nautical-style clock that rested beneath the picture.

The two women were very different in personality. Sylvia was an incurable optimist, a cheerful mender of fences. Betty had inherited something of her father's darker side. Things did not always work out, she knew; sometimes things went wrong.

Ed and Bob had gone that morning to McGuire Air Force Base in Trenton, New Jersey, where the show had originated that evening. They were flying back to the Bridgeport, Connecticut, airport where Ralph Cacace, the nightwatchman at the farm, was picking them up in Sullivan's new Lincoln. They should have been home by midnight.

Betty tried to think of something else. Bob was recently out of the Navy and Sullivan had persuaded him to have a go at television, so he had gone to work as a production assistant at CBS. Bob had thought he would like to get into the news end of things and Sullivan had made the appropriate introductions. Nothing had come of it, though, and Marlo Lewis, who was an executive producer at CBS as well as co-producer of the Sullivan show, agreed to take him on as a production assistant. Perhaps Sullivan leaned on Lewis a bit, but Marlo must have realized that he was driving the first nail into his own coffin. A son-in-law who knows the business is always more of a threat than one who doesn't. Still, the kid had a long way to go.

Betty shared another trait with her father; she was very sensitive to criticism. The jokes about her father's "stone-face" and awkward camera manner had hurt her deeply, more than she would ever admit. Now she was faced with the somewhat bitter sniping from old-timers on the show that Bob had gotten his job—as indeed he had—because he was the boss's son-in-law.

Bob was aware of the criticism, too, but he was determined to do a good job, learn the business, and bide his time. He plunged into work on shows like *The Verdict Is Yours,* with the genuine enthusiasm of one who was young and had no place to go but up.

"I hope nothing's wrong," Sylvia said.

"I'm sure the plane was just late getting in," Betty answered.

In her heart, she wasn't so sure. Her mind began to hear the ringing of the phone.

Shortly after two, the phone did ring. Betty felt the breath leave her body as if she had been punched hard in the chest.

There had been an accident, the voice said. Ed and Bob were hurt and had been taken to a hospital. There were no details about their conditions. A police car would come to take them to the hospital.

As the police car sped across the Connecticut countryside, Betty clung to her mother, who was in tears.

"They must be all right," Betty said. "They must be alive and conscious because one of them would have had to tell the police where to call and the number."

The police car roared into the emergency entrance of a local hospital only to have its occupants discover that they had come to the wrong hospital. Betty phoned the right hospital and had an awful moment of agony while she waited to hear the report. They were alive.

Sylvia was nearly hysterical by the time they arrived at Griffin Hospital in Derby and learned the details.

Sullivan had been driving the 1956 Lincoln along the winding Naugatuck Valley Road, about twelve miles from the Sullivan farm, when a 1953 Pontiac swerved into his lane and struck the Lincoln head-on.

"I thought to myself 'so this is how it is,'" Sullivan later said. He was thrown against the steering wheel and suffered a fractured seventh right rib, a slight cut on the nose, bruises of the back, and multiple cuts of the body and legs.

Bob, who was also riding in front, had a broken arm, a broken ankle and some deep face cuts. The driver of the Pontiac fractured his hip and jaw.

Most seriously injured of all was Cacace, the night watchman, with a skull fracture and chest injuries.

Sullivan was to relive the incident many times in his mind. He had been knocked unconscious and when he came to he was lying by the side of the road on a piece of tarpaulin. Bob and

Cacace were pinned in the wreck. He could taste blood in his mouth and his entire chest felt as if it had caved in. Somewhere in the distance he could hear the sound of sirens.

A man with a flashlight threw a beam directly in his face and said, "Hey, doc, come here quick. This one's Ed Sullivan."

"I don't know who he is," Sullivan heard the harried doctor say. "After a wreck like this, they all look alike."

A stranger, a man whom Sullivan had never seen before and never saw again, held his head on his lap while a young girl (he later found out that her name was Sue Miles) sat on the road next to him, holding his hand, unmindful of the blood that was staining her party dress.

Gasping for every breath, Sullivan asked the girl to phone Betty and Sylvia. "Tell them it's nothing serious," he murmered to her as she started off. It was she who gave the police the number to call.

Both cars were totally demolished in the crash.

Sullivan now had a legitimate first-hand reason to be proud of Lincoln-Mercury. If he had been driving a smaller car, he would almost certainly have been a dead man.

Sullivan was hospitalized for a few weeks after the crash. Sonny Werblin, now head of Madison Square Garden but then the head of the MCA talent agency and Sullivan's personal agent, dispatched two of his top underlings to Sullivan's bedside in case Ed should want something. One was Marty Kummer, the man who represented MCA clients to the Sullivan show on a week-to-week basis and the other was David Begelman, who later became president of Columbia Pictures before he was forced out in the "Hollywoodgate" scandal of 1977. Begelman was, and no doubt still is, a brilliant man, extremely fast on his feet.

Kummer and Begelman drove to the hospital in Connecticut and asked for Sullivan's room.

"No, no, no," the duty nurse said. "Mr. Sullivan cannot have any visitors. I'm sorry."

"I'm glad to see you're following my instructions," Begelman

130

said. "I'm Dr. Begelman, Mr. Sullivan's private physician, and this is my associate, Dr. Kummer. Would you call your chief of staff, please."

The startled nurse raced off and returned with the head of the hospital, who gave the two agents a grand tour of the facility, including the operating room, before depositing them at Sullivan's room. Through the whole thing, Kummer and Begelman avoided looking at each other for fear of breaking into hysterical laughter.

On another occasion, Begelman and Kummer used their ingenuity to lead Sullivan astray. Steve Lawrence and Eydie Gorme, not yet married, were starting to attract attention. Lawrence was an MCA client and he was growing increasingly annoyed because Eydie seemed to get a lot of nightclub work and he didn't. Kummer's secretary, who knew Eydie's manager, tipped Marty off that Lawrence was planning to leave MCA. Kummer told the secretary to tell Eydie that if Lawrence dropped MCA he, Kummer, would see that she didn't work the Sullivan show.

Sure enough, Lawrence left the agency and Kummer, who really couldn't prevent Sullivan from doing anything he wanted to, was faced with the task of following through on his threat.

The situation was complicated when Jerry Lewis headlined a big revue at the Palace and Eydie Gorme emerged as the real star of the show. She was knocking them dead, day in and day out. Sullivan decided he wanted to take a look at a German act called the Weir Brothers who, as fate would have it, came on right after Eydie.

"Jesus, Dave," Kummer told Begelman, "if Ed sees Eydie, he'll book her for eleven appearances."

"Leave it to me," Begelman said.

The day they were going to the show, Begelman made it a point to get to the theater a half-hour early. Sullivan was already there.

"Let's go in and have a look, Davie boy," Sullivan said. Begelman tried to stall but Ed started for the door. Eydie had just come on and was doing her big, brassy opening number, a throw-away, really, the low point of her act.

"What the hell is this?" Sullivan said.

"Oh, it's that fuckin' broad from the Bronx," Begelman said. "She's terrible."

"You're right," Sullivan answered. "Let's go downstairs and smoke."

It was to be another year before Sullivan "discovered" Gorme and presented her as the best young singer to come along in years.

Less than a year after the accident, Sullivan sold the farm. He confessed that he had never really liked the country much anyway. The crickets kept him awake. Besides, Bob and Betty had bought a house in Scarsdale which was country enough for their taste. The fact is, the accident had soured everyone on the idea of country living.

Sullivan sold the farm to the United Hotel Corporation of Las Vegas for $250,000 in the fall of 1957, more than twice what he had paid for it. It was a deal that caused tongues to begin wagging because shortly after the sale, Sullivan announced that he would be spending the month of July 1958 at the Desert Inn in Las Vegas. He would do a nightclub review there at $25,000 a week and, of course, the show would emanate from there.

One member of the production staff remembers being shocked by the news. "Ed had always said he would never play Las Vegas, that it simply wasn't his idea of a family kind of place. We were all very surprised until we found out that he had unloaded that farm on them. Then it all made sense."

Variety, the show business newspaper, hinted at the unusual nature of Sullivan's Vegas arrangement in several small items and its review of his first show from there began on an appropriately tongue-in-cheek note: "The Las Vegas Chamber of Commerce couldn't buy the kind of publicity given the gambling oasis by Ed Sullivan on his CBS-TVer last Sunday night. Sullivan, who's heading the Desert Inn show there, not only played up the local entertainment and betting angles, but also covered the more sedate aspects of daily living such as churchgoing and schooling. And the plug for the locale's new convention hall was really a wow."

Sullivan told *Variety* he was influenced to come to Las Vegas by two things: the excellent golf courses and "the fact that Jack Benny has played a Vegas saloon made it okay for me and my sponsors."

In any event, the Las Vegas group unloaded the farm at the bargain basement price of $50,000 less than a year after they bought it.

Whatever Sullivan's original objections to Las Vegas might have been, it was not a matter of personal morality. He was a regular, almost compulsive gambler. He had haunted race tracks all his life and for a brief period had even owned a few trotters.

He also loved craps and one summer in Miami, after the show had begun to catch on but before he had had a chance to make any real money from it, he dropped $10,000 in a night. That was considerably more than he had in the bank at the time.

An acquaintance loaned him money to pay the debt. As the years passed and Sullivan became more and more successful, the man waited for Sullivan to offer to repay the money. He never did and finally the man had to ask for it. An embarrassed Sullivan promptly paid up, but his interest in gambling was never the same again.

As for the accident, it was to have an important effect on the future of the show. During their respective recoveries, Sullivan was to get to know his son-in-law better. The youngster was coming along real well.

The Ed Sullivan Show
1956–1960

The period from 1956 to 1960 might best be described as the "age of culture" for *The Ed Sullivan Show*. Smarting from criticism that he had gone overboard on rock 'n' roll, Sullivan signed a contract with Rudolf Bing, general manager of the Metropolitan Opera, for scenes from five famous operas to be performed on the show on five different Sundays. The money involved was considerable—over $100,000—and so was the risk.

It was not Sullivan's first experiment with opera. Leading singers from the Met had made concert style appearances on the show for years and in 1953, Rise Stevens and Richard Tucker had done part of the last act of *Carmen* live from the Met stage on *Toast of the Town*. It was the first live broadcast from the Met, despite the claim of the Public Broadcasting Service that its 1977 opera telecasts had that distinction.

Sullivan was sure he had a winner with the first telecast. Maria Callas, already a legend, was to make her television debut in an eighteen-minute scene from *Tosca*.

That show was broadcast on November 25, 1956. Mme. Callas was in good form. Sullivan's audience, however, went away in droves. Over the eighteen-minute period, Sullivan lost six points in the Trendex ratings.

Sullivan knew he had a serious problem. Callas was his ace and he had already played it.

The second telecast—on January 27, 1957—featured Dorothy Kirsten and Mario Del Monaco in a scene from *Madame Butterfly*. This time enough of the audience disappeared to give Sullivan one of his rare ratings losses.

Clearly, something had to be done. Sullivan invited Rudolf Bing in for a chat. Jim Bishop, the writer, was there, and he recalled that Sullivan offered to use two more opera appearances instead of three and suggested they try a concert format. Bing, a man of formidable temper, rejected that idea and attempted to turn the blame back on Sullivan.

"I have seen two or three bad shows of yours," Bing said. "But this is none of my damned business. You control the show and it is always in the top two or three. . . . The only thing I criticize is your ventriloquists. I laugh two times. Three times. But when I see them seven times, that is too much. Use two, Ed. Cancel the last one. Then we are out of it."

And that's how Sullivan's fling with opera ended. On the fourth and last appearance on March 10, Renata Tebaldi and Richard Tucker sang a duet from *La Boheme*. They got four minutes—which was less than the commercials.

Much more successful was Sullivan's pursuit and eventual capture of the Russian Moiseyev Dance Troupe. By 1958, the Cold War had begun to thaw a little and the United States and the Soviet Union had launched a series of cultural exchanges. When Sullivan learned two months in advance that one of the world's great folk ballet companies would be in the United States that summer, he began an active campaign to land it for his show. Forgotten, it seemed, was his more or less rabid anti-communism of the early Fifties. More likely, he was beginning to fall under the moderating influence of his son-in-law Bob Precht, who spoke Russian and had a degree in international relations. Precht was assuming more and more responsibility around the show.

The Moiseyev appearance was a commercial and artistic success. Even though it was shown in black and white, the American public had never seen anything quite like it. The exuberance with which the Russians threw themselves into dance, the great height of their leaps, the dazzling spins, their uncanny precision, were a revelation to a public raised to believe that Russians were inferior at everything.

There was one anxious moment before the telecast. Sullivan dropped Arthur Leif, the American guest conductor of the Moiseyev, after he appeared before the House Un-American Activities Committee and refused to say if he was a member of the Communist Party. As if serving notice that by inviting the Russians to appear on his stage he had not gone soft, Sullivan said: "I've seen too many soldiers with feet severed, too many graves with helmets on them, to uphold and tolerate guys who won't take the oath of allegiance to our country."

In an ironic way, the great success of the Moiseyev appearance made Sullivan something of a hero in the communist world. On January 11, 1959, he scored his biggest journalistic coup by arranging one of the first American interviews with Dr. Fidel Castro, the leader of the Cuban revolution. How Sullivan managed to get to Castro even before the bearded leader made his triumphant entrance into Havana is an incredible tale.

On Monday morning, Clay Adams, a production manager at CBS, called director-cameraman Andrew Laszlo and told him to assemble a minimum crew for a location shoot with Ed Sullivan. He told Laszlo the destination was the Dominican Republic and that Sullivan planned to interview Dominican strongman Rafael Trujillo. Laszlo hired a young technician named Manny Alpert as his assistant and also added a

137

soundman. He then set about assembling the equipment he thought he would need. Since the interview would obviously take place at the presidential palace in Ciudad de Trujillo, Laszlo decided to take a large and bulky BNC (Blimp Noiseless Camera) of the type used in making Hollywood movies. He packed no hand-held or documentary equipment.

On Thursday afternoon, Laszlo, his crew, and Sullivan boarded a National Airlines plane bound—or so Laszlo thought—for the Dominican Republic. About a half-hour after takeoff, Sullivan moved over and sat down beside Laszlo.

"Anderooo," Sullivan said. "I've got to tell you something. We're not going to the Dominican Republic. We're going to Cuba to interview Fidel Castro. I didn't want to tell many people because it's going to be a big scoop."

Laszlo was shocked. "I must admit I was a little angry and put out," he says. "As far as I knew, the revolution wasn't a hundred percent over."

Laszlo told Sullivan that he would have to call his wife upon arrival to let her know where he was. Sullivan said not to worry; his office was calling all the wives.

That, as it turned out, was a fib.

The airport in Havana was an armed camp when the Sullivan group arrived. Gun-toting soldiers were everywhere. Sullivan was greeted by Jules Dubois, Latin American correspondent for the Chicago *Tribune*, the parent company of the *Daily News*. Dubois was liked and trusted by Castro and it was obviously he who had arranged the meeting.

Dubois explained that Castro was not yet in Havana but was in Matanzas, a city some sixty miles to the east, and was in the midst of one of his marathon speeches. He suggested that Sullivan should try to reach him there.

At this point, a man who said he was Castro's personal pilot staggered up, so drunk he could hardly walk, and offered to fly them there in a six-seat Beechcraft. Sullivan did some fast thinking and declined, saying that the equipment was too bulky

138

to fit in the plane. At this point, Dubois whispered some words to a couple of Fidelistas who disappeared and then came back a few minutes later with six commandeered taxi cabs.

And so they were off to Matanzas.

"It was a scary trip," Laszlo recalls. "Soldiers kept popping out of the darkness. The soldiers who were accompanying us had loaded and cocked machineguns and they kept falling asleep."

A few hours later, the Sullivan party arrived in Matanzas. At this point, Castro had already been speaking for three hours.

"I wondered where all the people were," Laszlo says. "Then we rounded a corner and came to the main square and there must have been 50,000 people there listening to Castro. It looked like a scene out of *Viva Zapata*."

Manny Alpert remembers it well, too. "We walked under the balcony where Castro was speaking and I remember looking up and seeing him there. It's something I'll never forget."

Once inside the building, Laszlo realized that his problems had only just begun. His equipment—obviously the wrong kind for the real assignment—was geared for 110 volts, 60 cycles. The building was not wired for that current.

"I was desperate," he says. "I really wasn't prepared at all and I had visions of going to Ed and saying we've come all this way and we just can't do it. I ran down the hall and discovered a miracle, an American-made watercooler. We ran all the cables to that one outlet."

Finally, Castro finished his speech and came into the room which was about 20 by 30 feet and contained at least a hundred people. Dubois managed to get enough of them out of the room to make space for the interview to take place.

"It took a while for the camera to get up to speed," Laszlo says, "and since the line was overloaded it was red hot. I was afraid some soldier was going to step on it and get electrocuted and then we'd all get executed."

Finally, though, the interview began. There was an anxious

139

moment when a soldier knocked over a light and it exploded, causing everyone with guns to reach for them nervously.

Sullivan looked slightly ill-at-ease among the dozens of earnest young men, all wearing combat fatigues, guns visible, amidst a cloud of cigar smoke.

Castro dominated the interview. Sullivan asked several questions and then said there were reports that Dr. Castro might be a communist. Was this true? Castro rolled his eyes, stroked his beard, and pointed to the religious medallions most of his men were wearing around their necks. "We are all Catholics," he said. "How could we be communists?" The logic of that seemed to stop Sullivan in his tracks. At this point, a soldier handed Castro a note. What it said was that Ché Guevara had arrived from Havana and wanted to see him. Castro stood up, said it was very late, that he was tired and going to bed.

"We loaded up all the equipment and headed back for Havana," Manny Alpert says. "Andy was still worried about whether the stuff we had shot was any good or not. The cables had gotten so hot that they fused right to the outlet."

After a few hours sleep in the Havana Hilton, Sullivan woke everybody up and said he wanted to get back as quickly as possible. They headed for the airport.

"It was an incredible madhouse at this point," Laszlo says. "People were trying to get out of the country and Castro's soldiers were trying to stem the tide. Ed saw George Raft, the actor, and went over to say hello. [Raft and certain other American "businessmen" are said to have lost fabulous gambling empires when Castro came to power.] Finally, we got started and we arrived back in New York on Friday evening. I went straight to the lab with the film because I knew I wouldn't be able to sleep until I knew if we had something or not. As it turned out, the quality really wasn't bad at all."

Sullivan showed the interview on Sunday night between a trained dog act and Alan King telling what really happens at suburban house parties.

It wasn't until a few months later, when Castro began to display his true political identity, that Sullivan realized that he had been duped. It shocked him to think that he might have been granted the interview because the communist world took him for a sympathizer, as a result of his booking of the Moiseyev troupe.

In August of that year, at the behest of the State Department, Sullivan took a troupe of performers to Russia for four weeks of performances in Moscow and Leningrad. The performers he chose were the usual something-for-everybody Sullivan vaudeville mix: Opera star Rise Stevens, dancers Marge and Gower Champion, accordionist Dick Contino, tap dancer Conrad ("Little Buck") Buckner, the Barry Sisters, illusionist Marvin Roy, tightrope walker Hubert Castle, and "for the Russian youngsters," a balloon act called The Shirleys and platespinner Erich Brenn.

Sullivan and his crew immediately ran afoul of the Russian bureaucracy. Shows were scheduled and cancelled without advance notice to the public. Bob Precht, who was directing the operation, wanted to take cameras into the streets and was continually denied permission to do so.

Finally, Sullivan had had enough. He dashed off an impassioned—not to mention, nasty—note to Nikita Khrushchev. The rotund Soviet premier, apparently liking Sullivan's straight-to-the-point style, promptly fired most of the Ministry of Culture. End of problems with bureaucrats. It may have been the first time in history that an American touched off a Soviet purge.

A few years later, Sullivan wrote about the Russian trip. What he had to say was revealing, not so much about the visit itself but about Ed Sullivan, the sentimentalist, the kid who read *Ivanhoe*:

In Moscow, we gave nightly outdoor performances at Green Theatre in Gorky Park. It seated 10,000, but starting with our opening night we played to 14,000

Russians. One night I secured 40 tickets for some visitors from the American College of Surgeons. Just before intermission, I told the Russian audience, through my interpreter, that sitting with them were these American doctors, emphasizing that our surgeons were in Russia to confer with Russian surgeons, for the benefit of all.

Russians are deeply emotional people and, when they heard this, it touched off a cheering demonstration that ever will be unforgettable. Each Russian family that attends a show brings along a small bouquet of flowers. At the end of an act, if they have enjoyed it deeply, a youngster representing the family walks right up on the stage and presents the flowers to the artist. On this night, unable to reach the American surgeons, the Russians threw these bouquets of flowers through the air at them. None of us had ever witnessed such a delighted turmoil.

Leningrad, because of its fantastically heroic defense of the city against the Nazis, occupies a special niche in the annals of Russian heroism. Opening one performance, tapdancing Conrad Buckner badly hurt himself in a prodigious leap from an elevation, climaxing in a sliding "split." His left heel apparently hit a board in the stage floor which was slightly higher than the rest. Two Russian women doctors who were in the audience rushed backstage, phoned for an ambulance and speeded him to a Leningrad hospital.

When they brought him back to the theater, young Buckner was on crutches but he insisted that he would appear in the finale, which was built around Rise Stevens singing "Getting to Know You" in Russian, At a certain musical cue, our entire cast joined her on stage, one half of the line of stars lifting small Russian flags above their heads and the other half of the line of stars lifting small American flags over their heads. As Miss Stevens sang her last note, I'd reveal a small Russian and a small American flag and cross the staffs of them, so that the flags were flying together.

This always exploded a storm of applause indicating the true feeling of the people of Russia, as contrasted to their Commie leaders.

On this particular night, because Buckner was standing on crutches, in the finale, I told the people of this city noted for heroism, pointing to Buckner, how deeply we appreciated the concern of the two Russian women doctors and how grateful all of us were for the expert care he had received in the hospital. And then I added:

I told Conrad not to come out in this finale but he said to me: "One does not come to Leningrad—to surrender."

Bedlam broke loose in the audience. Gower Champion told me later that even our performers were misty-eyed as they saw the Leningrad audience go wild. As the storm of applause died down, again through my interpreter I said to the audience:

"Because of the heroism of your city of Leningrad and because I have been told that each family in this city lost at least one man in the war, I'm certain that there is not a mother in Leningrad—just as there is not a mother in the United States—who ever again wants to send her husband or her son to war." Pandemonium broke loose. The audience surged forward to the orchestra pit. They threw kisses to the Americans on stage and they threw flowers. Women were weeping and dabbing their eyes with handkerchiefs. Some of them threw their arms around Elliot Lawrence. Others patted him on the back. These are the moments that you never forget.

Despite his many contacts with the Russians, though, Sullivan remained a fervent cold warrior. In 1961, this emotionalism involved him in one of the most unsavory episodes of his career.

Leon Bibb, an enormously talented black singer, had made five appearances on the show and was scheduled for a sixth. A man named Leslie Hoff, "Americanism" chairman of the Huntington, Long Island, American Legion Post, demanded, and got, a signed statement from Bibb repudiating the singer's prior associations with communist-front groups. The statement, drafted in Sullivan's theater office, said:

"The American Legion Post 60 of Huntington, New York, made a statement to the newspapers that I was a 'Communist sympathizer.' I labeled this accusation a lie.

"Publicly I wish to state that during my professional career I appeared repeatedly at communist front organizations and associated with known Communists. The American Legion states only the truth in their accusation of me, and I hereby freely and without coercion declare that I am fully divorced of all associations with the Communist Party. I fully denounce with deep conviction all organizations, persons, and associates affiliated with the Communist Party."

Two days later, Bibb retracted the statement and issued a new statement: "I was told to sign or else. I thought of my career first, but after thinking the whole situation over I find I cannot compromise my own convictions. I have never done anything detrimental to my country. By signing the statement I repudiated my own principles and beliefs that a man has the right to his own opinions and thoughts. . . . The American Legion's actions here are the antithesis of what Americanism really means."

It was an eloquent statement, one that Sullivan's father, the free thinker, would have applauded. Not so, his son.

"Bibb threw his career right out the window," Ed said. "I was shocked and mystified by the whole thing. I had taken a personal interest in this young man and I believed he was sincere when he signed the statement. I was prepared to have

144

him on my show again in February. But now he's really dug his grave. He won't be on our show and I don't think anybody else will touch him."

Sullivan was right about that. Bibb's career in this country was effectively over.

The Funny Men

Johnny Wayne and Frank Shuster are two of the funniest men
in the world. In Canada, which is where they've always lived
and, for the most part, worked, they are considered a national
treasure, only slightly less revered than Lord Stanley's Cup.
When Wayne and Shuster do a special for the CBC (four times
a year these days), most of Canada's twenty-three million
citizens drop what they're doing to watch.

They probably could have been institutions in the United
States, too, if they had chosen to come here and work, as some
younger Canadian comics like Rich Little and David Steinberg
have done. But Wayne and Shuster are Canadians to the core
and the fact of the matter is, most Americans care about
Canada only slightly more than they care about Mexico.

It is a little odd, then, that this Canadian duo should have
proved the most durable comedy act in the history of *The Ed
Sullivan Show*. Between 1958 and 1971, Wayne and Shuster
appeared on the show sixty-seven times. That is a record that
nobody else even approaches. They brought to the American

homescreen some of the most literate comedy ever seen here.

"I think Sullivan booked us originally because he was sick of hearing about us," Johnny Wayne, a spry, energetic man now in his late fifties, says. "Everywhere he went, he was always running into Canadians who would tell him he ought to get Wayne and Shuster for his show. Finally I guess he couldn't take it anymore and he arranged to look at one of our kinescopes."

Actually, it wasn't that difficult for Sullivan to find Wayne and Shuster. They were also represented by MCA. Sullivan liked what he saw very much, so much, in fact, that he did something he almost never did. He gave them carte blanche on material. Since some of their sketches ran fifteen to eighteen minutes, this was an extraordinary concession on his part.

"We were in Ed's office talking," Frank Shuster recalls, "and he was telling us not to change our style, that a lot of people would be trying to change us and that we should always resist because our humor was unique. He went on like that for awhile about resisting people who'd try to interfere and finally I said, 'Does this include a guy named Ed Sullivan?' That took him aback but after a few seconds he grinned kind of sheepishly and said, 'Yes, damn it. That means me, too.'"

Johnny and Frank had a tremendous advantage over the young comics for whom the Sullivan show was a make-or-break situation. If things didn't work out, they could always go back to being what they had been since the mid-Forties—Canada's best-loved comedians. Although Sullivan agreed to pay them his top price, money was no factor, either. They had made money in Canada, had come from well-off families (John's family had immigrated from Austria and Frank's from Holland), and John's father-in-law was quite wealthy. Neither was in any danger of starving.

They had gone to high school together in Toronto and then teamed up at the University of Toronto to star in the University Collegiate Follies. After that, they went into the Canadian Army together and were hustled off to Europe to entertain the troops. Their big break came in radio after the war when they were signed to do a Saturday night show following the incredibly popular *Bing Crosby Show.* Within six months, Wayne and Shuster were out-pointing Crosby. Their careers were launched.

Actually, the Sullivan show was not their first appearance on American television. In 1950, they came down to do a show called *Toni Twin Time.* John Wray, moonlighting from the Sullivan show, was director and Ray Bloch, also picking up some extra change, was the band leader. The host struck them as being a remarkably inept young man.

"A few weeks later, I was watching *The Kraft Theater* and I had to run to the phone and call Frank," Wayne says. "I said, 'Frank, remember that ass who hosted the show we did. He's on the Kraft show and he's the most brilliant goddamned comic actor I've ever seen.' It was Jack Lemmon."

John and Frank started doing television in Canada in 1953 and the immense following they had built up in radio simply followed them to the new medium. That gave them another advantage when they arrived at the Sullivan show five years later. Unlike comics who came to the show out of nightclubs, they were experienced television veterans.

Perhaps their most memorable sketch on the Sullivan show was the send-up of Julius Caesar called "Rinse the Blood Off My Toga." Wayne opens the sketch by saying: "I'm Flavius Maximus, private Roman eye. My license number is XIX-VIXXI. It also comes in handy as an eye chart. If you can't read it, you're nearsighted. If you can pronounce it, you're Polish."

The sketch gets wilder and wilder as Wayne attempts to solve the mystery of "Who killed Big Julie?" At one point he walks into a bar and orders a "martinus." "Don't you mean a martini," the bartender asks. "If I want two, I'll ask for them," Wayne shoots back. Later he draws his sword on a Roman soldier: "One false move and I'll fill you full of bronze."

The big moment comes when he encounters Caesar's widow, who happens to have a New York Jewish accent. "I said to him,

149

Julie don't go, I said. It's the Ides of March, already."

Another of their favorites was a bit about the star catcher of the Stratford baseball team who happens to be in a batting slump. Shuster plays the beleaguered coach and Wayne the unfortunate catcher. He opens the sketch in perfect Shakespearese: "Oh what a rogue and bush league slob am I who has ten days hitless gone."

At a later point, the umpire calls a foul ball. "So fair a foul I have not seen," Wayne says. "Get thee to an optometrist."

It was literate stuff and some of their friends in Canada had tried to persuade them not to do it on the Sullivan show. Pierre Burton, one of Canada's leading journalists and intellectuals, was one of them. "It's Shakespeare," he said. "The Americans will never get it."

While they were mulling that thought over, they happened into a diner for a cup of coffee. The guy behind the counter, a big bruiser with hairy arms, looked around from his task, which was flipping pancakes in the air and said, "Jeez, that baseball bit is really funny. You going to do it on the Sullivan show?"

Frank said they thought they might.

"I dunno," the cook said. "I don't think the Americans will get it."

Fortunately, John and Frank decided to do it anyway and the audience loved it. They walked offstage to a standing ovation. An American journalist in the wings asked John if they had done the sketch in Canada. John said yes.

"Did they get it?" the journalist asked.

Sullivan liked John and Frank better than most performers because they were not really show business types.

"All the big stars would be picked up in Rollses," John says, "and we'd go out front and there'd be Ed with a garment bag over his arm looking for a cab just like us. He was a very down-to-earth guy and I think it was a quality he admired in other people."

Because he had never worked on a show with animals before,

John was always fascinated by the menagerie that Sullivan assembled backstage.

"The elephants were the worst," he says. "Just mean animals. Every once in a while you would hear a stagehand scream because some elephant had pinned him against the wall. Oh, and I remember being in an agent's office once when somebody from the Sullivan show called and wanted to get a bear. 'Who do you want,' the agent said, 'Mr. Charlie or Bobo?' 'What's the difference?' the guy from the Sullivan show said. 'Are you kidding,' the agent said, 'Mr. Charlie is a *name* bear.'

"Another time I was sitting out front with Mark Leddy during rehearsal and this elephant let go—I mean, it was a vicious crap. Mark didn't miss a beat or even turn his head. 'Wouldn't take many of those to make a dozen,' he said."

Although they built up a large following in the U.S. and were often pressured by their agents to move down, Wayne and Shuster simply never felt any particular need to conquer their neighbors to the south. They were both family men and Toronto is where they wanted to stay.

Wayne has three sons. One is an instructor at Yale in, of all things, American history, particularly the South; another is a contributing editor of *The Financial Post*, Canada's leading business newspaper, and the third was most recently an associate producer of *Hockey Night in Canada*.

Shuster's daughter, Rosie, is a writer on *Saturday Night Live*, the incredibly popular American show, and—although they are separated—is married to Lorne Michaels, the producer. Shuster's son is just starting to enjoy some success as a comedian.

Over the years, Wayne and Shuster remained close to the people of the Sullivan show. When John Wray left the show, for example, they brought him to Canada to direct their program.

"Johnny was one of the coolest guys in the world," Wayne says. "I remember once Sullivan wanted to have on an Olympic figure skating champion—I think it was Dick Button. The problem was where to get the ice. It was finally decided that

151

they would switch to Madison Square Garden during the intermission of a New York Rangers hockey game and Button would do his thing. Well, it was a really brutal game—the Rangers and the Black Hawks were pounding the shit out of each other. Finally, though, they leave the ice after the first period and Sullivan cuts to the Garden and the music comes up and Button skates out and starts doing these elegant swirls. Well, the crowd didn't know what the hell was happening and they start booing and throwing things. This was live, remember. Johnny is in the control room when suddenly he hears this voice booming through the audio from the Garden: 'Get that fuckin' fag off the ice.' He doesn't bat an eye, just turns to his assistant and says very calmly, 'Perhaps we should turn off the audio.'"

Wayne says he had no regrets that he and Shuster never really attempted to make the transition to the United States.

"I remember an agent came up to see us once and he said you guys have just got to move down. You're hot and I can get you a lot of work. We said what we always did which is we were born and grew up in Canada, we liked it here, and we're happy. I'll never forget what the poor guy's answer was. He looked me straight in the eye and said: 'Yeah, but happiness isn't everything.'"

152

The Ed Sullivan Show
1960–1964

The beginning of the 1960 season brought many changes to *The Ed Sullivan Show*. To the surprise of almost no one, Marlo Lewis—who had shared the co-producer title with Sullivan from the beginning—decided to leave the show. The official reason he gave is that he planned to take it easy and write a book. The real reason is that Sullivan felt it was time to make room for his son-in-law, Bob Precht.

Precht, then twenty-nine, had been assuming more and more control of the show, anyway. It was he who produced the show's on-location programs from Russia, Alaska, Portugal, and elsewhere.

Sullivan picked a good time to make the change. The show had been slipping badly in the ratings and it obviously needed an infusion of fresh blood. No one at CBS could fault him for that.

"I'm not sure I forced Marlo out," Precht says, "although I obviously felt I was ready for the job. When you're twenty-nine, you think you can do anything. I got along well with

Marlo; he helped me a great deal when I was learning the business. I think there might have been some bad feeling between Ed and Marlo over the change, but I was not directly involved in it."

Although Marlo declines to discuss his departure, other than to say that the decision to leave was entirely his own, other insiders say Marlo felt he really had no choice.

The accession of Precht, though long expected, sent a wave of panic through the Sullivan pioneers. Bob owed no allegiances to the old ways of doing things. He was young, ambitious, and—by most accounts—nearly as cold-blooded as Sullivan himself. Clearly, some changes would be made.

Long-time director John Wray was, and is, one of the most skeptical. "Precht was strictly from amateur night," Wray says. "He would have been lucky to get a job in the mailroom if he hadn't been the boss's son-in-law."

Marlo was not one of those who joined in the son-in-law remarks. He himself had married the daughter of the president of the Blaine-Thompson Advertising Agency and had once worked for his father-in-law.

To this day, there are survivors from the early years who blame Precht for the show's demise. Forgotten, apparently, is the fact that the show ran another eleven years after he took over—only a year less than it ran without him.

A less impassioned look at the facts might even lead one to believe that Precht actually saved the show and that his innovations were largely responsible for its continued success, albeit at a level somewhat below its peak years. Certainly the show he inherited had become an antique. The old vaudeville look far outweighed any television production values the staff tried to give it.

Precht almost immediately made the show look better by bringing in a new designer and by moving performers into sets, rather than having them do their acts before a plain curtain. He also brought a certain order to the chaotic way the show was put together.

"I was always appalled at how little time Ed left before the show to put the pieces back together," Precht says. "Everything was always left until the last minute. I tried to build more flexibility into the production, working out shots with cameras in advance, that sort of thing."

Precht also began bringing in—gradually, over a period of time—his own production people. Despite Sullivan's strengths as a booker of talent and Lewis's knowledge of music and dance, neither was particularly adept at running a production staff.

Under Marlo's command, the show was almost literally thrown together in a seven-hour period on Sundays. Staff members in the control room would listen to the New York Giants football games during rehearsals. Singers who couldn't quite figure out why Ray Bloch, the orchestra leader, wasn't keeping time with their songs didn't realize that under the headsets he wore he was really listening to the exploits of Frank Gifford and Sam Huff.

Precht put an immediate end to the football games and started taking time on Saturdays to block out camera shots and rehearse some of the more difficult numbers.

Bob also learned to worry a lot. On a Sunday when Richard Burton was scheduled to appear in a scene from *Camelot*, he had someone from the production staff call almost hourly to make sure Burton was still sober enough to go on.

In direct contrast to the Sullivan old guard, most of whom had come into television from Broadway or vaudeville, Precht's charges were mostly young, bright college graduates whose sole experience was the television medium.

Typical of the kind of person Precht was looking for was Bill Bohnert, a twenty-seven-year-old set designer who arrived on the scene in 1960 armed with a degree in architecture from MIT and an MFA from Yale. A week after Bohnert was hired by CBS to work on the Sullivan show as assistant set designer, Grover Cole, the head set designer, was hospitalized. When Cole returned, he found himself sharing responsibility with the

155

newcomer and by the end of the next season Cole was out completely. Bohnert remained with the show until its demise.

"Bob made a definite effort to modernize the show," Bohnert says. "There had never been much emphasis on sets before. Performers simply did their acts before a curtain. It's interesting because people had such a strong image of that curtain that when I would say that I designed sets for the Sullivan show, they would say 'Does the Sullivan show have sets?' This went on for years after we stopped doing the curtain bit.

"I found live television to be a marvelous training ground. Set changes had to be done in seconds. Sometimes Ed would book an act at the last minute simply because they happened to be in the news and we would have to create a set overnight. It was like working in a state of perpetual controlled crisis. Your adrenalin was flowing all the time. The interesting thing was that people really did work together. There was no time for the kind of petty jealousies that you often find among people working on a show. It was a kind of exercise in group survival."

Things did not go so smoothly during the first two years of Precht's reign, however. Sullivan himself took a more active interest in the production aspects of the show than he had during the last few years under Marlo Lewis. Precht resented this attention. Tempers were frequently short in those days and Precht clashed often with some of the old-timers. He was careful not to antagonize Sullivan directly, however. "Ed would have chewed him up and spit him out," observed one Sullivan crony, perhaps wistfully.

Still, Precht had the kind of youthful courage that only a young man with an important job and a lot to prove can summon. After weeks of brooding and making life miserable for Betty and the kids at home, he finally marched into Sullivan's office one day and informed Ed that he didn't want to be co-producer of the show, he wanted to be producer. Not only that, he wanted to have a say in the bookings.

"It was difficult for Ed, particularly sharing responsibility for bookings," Precht says. "Marlo always got the lineup over the telephone. I just felt that if I was going to be producer, then I wanted to have the job as well as the title. It was really hard for him to give the responsibility over because he was not at a stage where he really wanted to. I felt that some of the bookings were getting detrimental to the show. I mean, how do you use a Jack Carter six times in a season? Ed finally agreed, though, and he was pretty gracious about it."

Precht was smart enough not to try to totally clean house in the beginning. If he thought John Wray was not a good director, he simply bided his time until the opportunity presented itself. Like most strong-willed people, Ed was not easily bullied, but—once one caught on a bit—he was fairly easily manipulated.

Precht's promotion was not the only big change at the beginning of the 1960 season. Lincoln-Mercury dropped its sponsorship of the show at the end of 1959, citing the high costs involved. The automobile makers had been contributing $5 million of the $10 million annual tab for the show. Sullivan was just as glad to see them go. His continued use and support of black performers at a time when the civil rights struggle was heating up had annoyed many dealers around the country. Their annoyance, in turn, infuriated Sullivan. He had been working with black performers since 1930. He had no intention of stopping now.

There was another, more practical, factor, also. Perhaps it was the influence of Bob Precht (who was a far better businessman than Ed), but Sullivan became interested in money in a serious way. With the help of his lawyer Arnold Grant and his agents at MCA, he had worked out a deal for Revlon to become sponsor of the show. In return, Sullivan would become an officer of the cosmetic company with all the perquisites that such a deal might entail.

The problem was that Sullivan was in no position to close the deal. He did not own the show; CBS did. Any arrangement Sullivan made would have to have CBS's blessing.

Meanwhile, CBS president Frank Stanton emerged from a

separate huddle with Colgate chairman Ed Little and announced that the new half-sponsor of the Sullivan show would be none other than Sullivan's old enemy, Colgate-Palmolive, a company that had spent more than $50 million at NBC over the years trying to knock him off the air.

Sullivan was understandably furious. After a frantic conference with CBS executives—during which his salary and deferred compensation arrangements were hiked considerably—Sullivan emerged and announced that he could "live with" the Colgate arrangement.

While Sullivan fumed, Bob Precht made a note to himself to start looking for a way to wrest control of the show from CBS. An independent production company was the answer but he would wait for the opportunity.

Sullivan never forgave Frank Stanton, however. Eight years later, while the show was still running on CBS, Sullivan opened up on his old nemesis in an interview in *Look:*

"Once when I had accumulated some money, I decided to invest it. I didn't have the slightest idea how to do it—so I went to Frank Stanton for help—after all, he practically invented CBS so he knew how to make money. Bill Paley is a great friend of mine and a genius, but Stanton knows money. The guy was ice cold. He's a sort of hopeless case as a human, and a success as a machine. He just looked at me."

Sullivan went on to add that all the presidents of CBS he had encountered—with the exception of Jack Schneider—had been "ungrateful, impolite people."

"I've never heard anything vaguely approaching 'thank you' or 'good job.' I never even heard from Stanton on the show's anniversaries. When you consider the money I've made for CBS. We've kept their Sunday night supremacy going for years, the strength we've provided for the programs that precede and follow us, the performers who worked here first and then on to their own CBS show. It's selfish and bad manners. At first I was hurt, but now I don't give a damn. I know them for what they are, and my relationship with CBS presidents is strictly business. Thank God Bill Paley isn't at all like the rest of the jerks in that mausoleum."

It was strong stuff but by then, 1968, Sullivan could afford to be feisty with CBS. Thanks mainly to the good business sense of Bob Precht, he then owned the show. Sullivan Productions had been formed in 1964 with Ed and Sylvia holding fifty-one percent and Bob and Betty forty-nine percent. Precht had also steered the company into other investments; a cable TV company in Illinois, for example.

But Precht's influence began slowly. Little by little, bookings for the Sullivan show began to reflect Precht's more liberal tastes. In 1963, Sullivan and Precht engaged a young folk singer named Bob Dylan. CBS killed the appearance after it learned that Dylan planned to sing "The Talking John Birch Society Blues." Sullivan blasted CBS for the decision.

Precht was a great fan of social and political satire and in 1963, he steered the Sullivan show into one of its most noble experiments. He booked a few segments of a revue called "What's Going on Here?" featuring the top talents of Britain's theatrical hit *Beyond the Fringe* and *The Establishment,* along with Bob and Ray, the fine American comedy team.

To viewers accustomed to the usual Sullivan vaudeville fare, the "What's Going on Here?" sketches must have seemed strange, indeed. The format, staged by Jonathan Miller of *Beyond the Fringe,* was brilliant. Bob and Ray acted as an anchor news team for the bits, most of which were in TV news format and based on current headlines. Ray announced he would be "mother-henning" the land masses of the globe (which he promptly peeled off a world globe prop) and Bob would be handling the water masses ("under, over, around, and through").

They then exchanged headline items; "Fidel Castro is accusing the CIA of launching hurricane Flora. It was last seen heading for Red China," and "Alabama has moved ahead of Mississippi in the race race."

Peter Cook did a burlesque of a Scotland Yard inspector

investigating the great train robbery and showed a composite drawing of the "mindermast," which was, in fact, a drawing of the Archbishop of Canterbury. Black comedian Godfrey Cambridge did a bristling bit about a civil-rights-struck citizen (the Lincoln-Mercury dealers—though departed—must have loved that one).

By far the most memorable sketch, however, was an interview on Vietnam between Jeremy Geidt and John Bird which was total double-talk. It was followed by a film clip of President Kennedy in a press conference mumbling a jargon that was a straight replica of the Geidt-Bird dialogue. This was 1963, when most of the American public still favored United States involvement in Vietnam. Clearly, it was the first anti-Vietnam sketch presented on American television.

Sullivan took some of the spark out of the bit by remarking that the White House had granted permission for use of the Kennedy footage. Still, it was there and it was pointed. (Several years later, on the same network, the Smothers Brothers were to get in trouble over much less.)

Precht often declines to take much credit for innovations such as this experiment with satire—perhaps because the shows alienated more people than they won over—but clearly the inspiration was his.

One of the major reasons Precht was able to exert so much influence over the show right from the beginning was Sullivan's declining health. His ulcer had reached a critical point by the summer of 1960 and he had had it removed. Still, his health had lagged for months after the operation and eventually he was forced to go to the Mayo Clinic for follow-up gall bladder surgery. All this meant more work, and more influence, for Precht.

Despite his failing health, Sullivan was still a battler. In the spring of 1961, he became involved in what was to be one of his most celebrated run-ins. His antagonist was Jack Paar and the issue was money paid to guest stars.

Guests on the Sullivan show were now getting up to $10,000 an appearance while Paar was paying many of the same people the union minimum of $320 for his late night show. For some reason or other, Sullivan hadn't noticed. On March 8, 1961, he did.

Actually, the whole thing came about because Sullivan didn't have much to do at the time. This was during the midst of Bob's assertion of authority and Sullivan was making a real effort to stay out of his hair.

A couple of months earlier, Marty Kummer had sold a young Canadian singer named Joan Fairfax to Sullivan. A few days before the appearance, another singer, better known, became available and Fairfax was bumped from the show and re-scheduled. As fate would have it, the new date was within a few days of an appearance Kummer had scheduled for her on the Paar show. He told Sullivan, who said that it was all right for her to make the appearance. Something happened and she was bumped from the Sullivan show again and rescheduled a second time. Meanwhile, she had done the Paar show and was a hit. Jack invited her back. Although the appearances were only one day apart, Kummer didn't tell Sullivan this time because he figured he already had his okay. It was an oversight that would cause him to be fired and re-hired by both Sullivan and Paar over the next few weeks.

Fairfax appeared on the Sullivan show on March 5 for $1,000 and the Paar show the following night for $320. On Wednesday, Sullivan was bored and at home at the Delmonico and he did something he almost never did—he started to read some fan mail. About the third envelope he opened said: "How come Joan Fairfax looked so much better on the Paar show than she did on your show?" He hit the roof.

Kummer and Bob Precht were having lunch at Sardi's East when the phone rang. Marty took the call. Sullivan began by casting certain aspersions on Kummer's family background and gradually working himself up to suggesting certain quaint anatomical impossibilities that Marty might attempt.

Sullivan vowed to get to the bottom of this matter.

He was amazed to learn that two of his brightest stars, Myron Cohen and Sam Levenson, had also been frequent guests for the minimum wage on the Paar program.

Sullivan felt that Fairfax and the others were violating the "exclusivity clause" standard in the industry which forbade performers to appear on other programs three weeks before and one week after the Sullivan show without permission.

Although he was angry, Sullivan's feelings about Paar were not personal. Four years before, when Paar had been cancelled by CBS, he had been invited to come on the Sullivan show "as often as he wanted" for $5,000 an appearance. However, the fee question was a professional matter and Sullivan notified talent agents that performers who did the Paar show for $320 would get the same when they showed up at his show. This injunction, he said, did not apply to newcomers or established stars who simply talked with Paar but did not perform.

The first result of Sullivan's phone calls was that Myron Cohen cancelled a scheduled appearance on the Paar show on March 9. That night, Paar—on the verge of tears, as he frequently was—read an "open letter" to Sullivan on the air:

Dear Ed: I don't think you could have struck any blow that would injure the medium that glorifies you more than the ultimatum you gave television talent today. First of all, I am appalled that you raised the question of money and that you challenge me to pay performers what you pay them. Ed, I don't have money to pay performers. This show is a low-budget freak that caught on because performers want to come on and want time to entertain people without the monkey act and the Japanese jugglers waiting in the wings.

The studio audience laughed.

He said that challenging Sullivan was a strain because of the favor Ed had done for him four years before. "Believe me, I'll never forget you helped me when I really needed it. But I've got to level with you, Ed. I made more in those four minutes on your show than I make now in a whole week and I'm kind of a hit now.

"You and I aren't even competing, Ed. As a matter of fact, I'll tell you something. Four years ago when this show started to catch on, NBC was running Steve Allen against you on Sunday nights and they offered me big money to appear on Steve's show to help build a rating against you. But I refused repeatedly because I can't be bought, Ed, nor can my loyalty to a friend. And though now may be a strange time to bring it up I would never do anything to hurt a friend, Ed—four years ago or now.

"If you are able to economically frighten performers off this show, where are you going to find the Bob Newharts who we brought to television, or the next Mike and Elaine you first saw here? Or the Pat Suzuki we found for you? Or Shelley Berman? Where are the Genevieves, the Carol Burnetts, the Earl Grants, the Phyllis Dillers? Believe me, Ed, I want Pat Suzuki to get five thousand dollars from you—nothing could please me more. But it's the three hundred and twenty dollars here that made the five thousand dollars possible for so many.

"Ed Sullivan, I am now going to ask NBC for the Sunday night time eight-to-nine opposite you at least one week and, Ed Sullivan, I want you to pick the week you have booked the finest, the best talent that you can get on that show. And that's considerable. It'll be great fun for the audience and we can turn over our entire salaries to the AFTRA (American Federation of Television and Radio Artists) Welfare Fund."

Paar told the audience: "All of you in a way can vote. Watch the show you want to watch, and maybe I'll learn a terrible lesson. . . . But it would be fun, Ed, wouldn't it? C'mon, old boy!"

Sullivan replied, "I think Paar owes me $320. It's the best show he's had in weeks."

He wired Paar, challenging him to: "A debate of the issues

163

involved . . . tonight, tomorrow, or any night mutually agreeable on the *Tonight* show because the format is more suited to our purpose." He made one stipulation: "So that your national audience can hear each point clearly, let us agree to ban any studio audience."

Paar answered:

"I am happy to welcome you on the *Tonight* show where you will be given every courtesy we have already extended to President Kennedy, Billy Graham, Vice President Nixon, and a host of other guests who have found in our low-budget atmosphere an opportunity to be seen at their informal, relaxed best without limitation of time. However, since none of these mentioned nor any other person who ever appeared requested that people be banned from attending, I feel I must refuse your petition that our meeting be unattended by the live presence of an audience. If the ground rules are to be fair play, I feel any discussion of what will affect the future entertainment of millions of viewers, yours and mine, must be attended, by representatives of the people. Looking forward to seeing you at your convenience, I only hope that your appearance on our show for scale will not ban you from your own. Regards. . . ."

It was a slow news week and the feud had become the number one story in the country. Both Sullivan and Paar—emotional men if ever there were such creatures—seemed to be enjoying all the attention and publicity immensely.

On March 10, Sullivan sent the press a copy of a telegram he had wired Paar:

Dear Jack, Let us direct our debate on important principles to the intellect of your millions of TV viewers rather than to the comparatively small studio audience which nightly responds to your skillful cues with cheers or boos. This could be most disconcerting to me as well as to our TV listeners. I am sure you will agree with me, Jack, that our debate is the most important thing rather than the studio sound effects. I'm counting on you to wire your acceptance of this on the basis of good sportsmanship.

Sincerely, Ed Sullivan

Paar taped an answer which was inserted into that night's show: "This is Jack Paar speaking to you by telephone from my home. I am phoning this message to be played in tonight's repeat show. . . . I think that Ed Sullivan is wrong in a democratic country to give an ultimatum to actors that they could work on one show or another because economically that is what is going to happen. . . . There is going to be an audience every night I am here—Monday, Tuesday, Wednesday. I am not going to change this show for Ed Sullivan. The audience will be the same audience that has requested tickets two months ago. I will see that no one in the next week can get any extra tickets—no page boys, no press photographers, no sponsors. Further, Ed and I will walk out together. There will be nobody to speak before the other. The third thing, I insist humbly that Ed speak first and last.

"Fourth, I suggest that Ed bring his own moderator, his closest friend, his lawyer, anyone he wants to bring. . . . I'm perfectly willing to go on Sullivan's show before an audience or without an audience . . . on only one provision—and that is that some time be given to the issues that he has raised. I don't want to be given four minutes and then have eight acrobats come on in the middle of the discussion."

Sullivan wired his acceptance:

Relying on assurances from NBC-TV and Paar about the debate which I have proposed, I will waive my insistence on the elimination of Paar's studio audience at the video taping of our debate. I have been told that there will be no audience rudeness such as disturbed Chicago newspapermen Irv Kupcinet and the New York *Herald-Tribune*'s Hy

Gardner when they were invited to his show for a question-and-answer session.

The big "debate" was set for Monday, March 13. Seldom in the history of television had so little an issue become such an incredible publicity event.

That day Bob Precht and Paul Orr, Parr's producer, and NBC vice-president Jim Stabile met in Bennett Cerf's office to make arrangements for the debate. At Paar's request reporters were to be barred from the audience, although they could watch the taping on a monitor in a private room. Sullivan would speak first. Paar would present his rebuttal, then Sullivan would have another chance to speak. Cerf, as moderator, would open and close the half-hour session. Afterward Paar and Sullivan would exit separately. Then Hugh Downs, Paar's announcer, would take over the show for the remaining period. Paar had agreed there would be no mention of the debate on the program that followed.

Sullivan understood it would be a debate, not a discussion, and continued preparing his remarks. At 2:30 P.M. Paar's office notified him that Paar insisted on a discussion. Sullivan refused.

He wired the press:

"Jack Paar, through his representatives, has just called off tonight's debate. Paar simply has welched. As a matter of record I challenged Paar to this debate last week. He specifically accepted the debate. This morning in the presence of moderator Bennett Cerf at Random House, Paar's attorney, James Stabile, acknowledged that the word "debate" means that each side in turn presents his argument and that the first speaker ends the debate with rebuttal. The other day Paar in newspapers insisted that I speak first and that I speak last. I agreed to this. Paar has now said that he will not appear unless I agree that following the debate we will have a discussion. Obviously, after the debate I'd have nothing to discuss with Paar and there would be no subject open to discuss. I am ready

166

to go on tonight and debate. If Paar wants to change his mind before 4 P.M. I will go on. Paar can now put up or shut up and his deadline is now 4 P.M. I have no further comment."

The wire was sent at 3:28 P.M. NBC responded with a lengthy statement saying, in essence, that "Sullivan bowed out."

Sullivan said, "The welcher's deadline expired at four o'clock. Paar simply has welched. . . . I refused a discussion because I have nothing to discuss. . . . When Paar was notified, he immediately choked up and started to pull his crying bit. You know the old vaudeville routine of bringing your wife and children onstage when your act stinks. . . . He's overflowing with emotion. Now he wants to get into a loveseat with me after the debate. He told me I could make the ground rules and now he's trying to tell me what they'll be. . . .

"Paar is a welcher. He is a hell of a shadow-boxer, but I think he chokes up when he realizes the time has come to stand up and debate. I was all set. My makeup man was already here in my office but Paar realized that he didn't have a leg to stand on. . . . My wife and I turned down front-row seats to the Patterson-Johansson fight in Miami Beach for this. . . . That's the thing that really burns me up."

Paar said, "Sullivan has backed out. He would not agree to a free and open discussion of the issues, the only condition I made and the only democratic way of clearing up the whole mess. Heck, I agreed to everything else: that he choose the moderator, that he bring his own make up man, that he have the use of the teleprompter, that he stand centerstage, that there be only three-quarter length shots of him, that there be no reaction shots, that he appear first and last. Obviously, he was looking for an out."

That night, Paar opened a fifteen-minute monologue by saying, "Ed Sullivan has proved to be as honest as he is talented."

He said he "never felt more melancholy" and was disappointed in Sullivan "as a man."

"I think I'm as normal and decent a person as you'll find in show business. . . . I do not enjoy what I am about to do to Mr. Sullivan." What he did was call him "The Masked Marvel" and tell the audience Sullivan asked for a teleprompter and "any idiot can read a teleprompter."

"He is afraid to appear on the show—not that he would be murdered, but that he would commit suicide in front of an audience. . . . Everybody looks more interesting here, and if you had been here, Ed, you might have looked more interesting for the first time."

Paar continued: "Why would you [the audience] be rigged? Mr. Sullivan implies that you are rigged. I wonder how those tennis players and golf players and those movie actors who stand up in the audience. . . . I wonder if they just happen to be there. . . . Sullivan perhaps rigs his audience.

"A debate means we discuss it, that we argue if you like, that we ask each other questions, that I present a few little things to Mr. Sullivan about his past operations, about how financially he has run that show, about the people he has conned, about the way he has used his column to beat people over the head who could not come on his show. This is what I wanted to discuss because this is what is behind it all. . . .

"I am not going to fool around much longer about how I feel about Mr. Sullivan because he has made a very difficult decision performers must decide, a loyalty which is unnecessary. I don't want my friends to have to decide between Ed Sullivan's money or my friendship or loyalty or enthusiasm for them. . . . They are apparently going through a heck of an experience and I do not want them to have to decide such a very important decision.

"Ed Sullivan is a liar. That is libel. He must now sue and he must go to court—and not like·Winchell and Hoffa, who sue just to save their face. The public is going to insist you go to court and under oath, I repeat, Ed Sullivan, you lied today."

On Tuesday morning *The New York Times* printed a critical editorial by Jack Gould entitled "Highly Distasteful Brawl." It was harsh and it had the effect of sobering up both combatants.

"At a time when the rest of the world is concerned over grave issues, the United States presents the spectacle of two grown men, each enjoying an annual income well up in six figures, regaling millions of their fellow citizens with allegations and innuendos about each other. . . . The emergence of the dispute emphasizes the almost incredible pressures that are a daily part of the TV life. The fierceness of the constant fight for survival in video is indicative of how the law of the jungle devours many otherwise sensible people and directly affects what the public sees.

"Hours of time on television and eight-column streamers in the newspapers for the Messrs. Paar and Sullivan? If the people of the Congo think we have gone back to the playpen, they can't be blamed."

CBS sent out a wire with Ed Sullivan's final statement:

Before planing today to Miami to fulfill a long-standing engagement to emcee a charity show for crippled children, Ed Sullivan issued this statement: "Paar's intemperate display on his show last night indicated how wise we were in insisting on a formal debate from which he withdrew. Paar proved last night that he did not intend at any time to debate the issue and that his demand for a discussion instead of debate only was a cloak for exactly what he did last night: name-calling, a shocking indulgence in personalities, and a continued willful distortion of the true issue.

"For thirteen years, I have attempted to present wholesome entertainment for the entire family. I stand on this record. This controversy, as Paar's behavior proved last night, is clearly a misuse and an abuse of the airways and has become objectionable to the public. Consequently, I will have nothing more to say on this subject."

The feud simply died then, although Sullivan revived it briefly in 1967 when he told *Time* magazine that the best he could say for Paar was that he is "a thoroughly no-good son of a bitch. That's spelled s–o–n. . . ."

Paar's response was printed in the *Time* "Letters to the Editor" column:

> In your article on "Variety Shows" (Oct. 13), Ed Sullivan referred to me as a "thoroughly no-good son of a bitch." Mr. Sullivan always had trouble with the truth and I have a birth certificate to prove him false again. Furthermore, I state as a sworn fact that Ed Sullivan's office has called my agent on at least four or five occasions in the past year to get me to do a television special in cooperation with his company; and are you ready for one of the subjects that he chose for me? The Vatican. I declined.

Paar made an on-the-air reply on Lee Bailey's half-hour interview program, "Good Company." It was very funny. "Ed is not noted for his use of language. It's not his strong point. His strong point is singing and dancing and we all remember and love Ed when he used to put his feet over the footlights and sing 'Over the Rainbow'. . . . I don't know why he said it unless he was trying to prove at his age some kind of manhood. . . . NBC has its peacock and I think that CBS now has its cuckoo. . . . Ed Sullivan is the best thing on his show. . . . It's probably the miracle of all of show business. . . . Who can bring to a simple English sentence such suspense and mystery and drama? . . . Who but Ed Sullivan can introduce a basketball player with the reverence once reserved for Dr. Schweitzer?"

Afterward Sullivan said, "I regret having said it, [that Paar was a son of a bitch]. It was a flare-up. I wish we could turn the calendar back. I wish it hadn't occurred. You just shouldn't pop off like that. . . . Paar is a damn talented guy." Then he wrote Paar a personal letter and expressed the same sentiment. Paar wrote a warm letter back and the feud was over.

170

Although it received no publicity at the time, Sullivan was also putting the heat on another, younger rival, Dick Clark. Clark, who had established himself with *American Bandstand,* had been given a Saturday night variety show on ABC. As Clark recalled in his memoirs, *Rock, Roll & Remember:*

"He was a miserable bastard in those days. He tried to do us in, to kill the show. He tried to put clauses in his contracts that if an artist did his show the artist couldn't appear on any other show a week before and eight days after their appearance on his show. He couldn't understand how artists like Tony Bennett did my show for $155, then hit him for $5,000 to $7,000 for an appearance on his show. He was convinced I put a pistol to Tony's head. Sullivan didn't understand that *Bandstand* and the Saturday night show with their huge teen-age audiences sold records."

According to Clark, Sullivan took the issue to AFTRA and tried to establish that Clark was pressuring acts into appearing on his show—an interesting irony since Sullivan himself had often been accused of doing just that.

Clark says he wrote Sullivan pleading letters. "I wanted his acceptance and his blessing," he says. It was to be ten years, though, before the men met and became friends.

Interestingly enough, Clark launched a new variety series during the 1978 television season patterned somewhat on the Sullivan format. Three former key members of the Sullivan production staff worked on the special which launched Clark's new series.

The emotional strain of the Paar affair had left Sullivan drained and exhausted. He was not recovering from his ulcer surgery as quickly as doctors had hoped—mainly because he still needed gall bladder surgery. Precht had taken the opportunity presented by Sullivan's illness to insist that they begin taping some shows to present during the summer. No reasonable person, he argued, could present fifty-two hours of live television year-in, year-out without damaging his health, or sanity, or both. Ed finally, reluctantly, agreed.

Precht also won another concession at the end of the 1962 season. John Wray, director for thirteen years and a frequent target of Bob's wrath, had to go. Sullivan detested the idea, but he sensed Bob's urgency and he was anxious to back his son-in-law in what had developed into a major test of strength.

It was particularly difficult for Sullivan because he genuinely liked Wray and had said on several occasions, "You're my director as long as I'm on the air."

In the summer of 1961, while Sullivan was in Japan, Precht fired Wray and replaced him with Tim Kiley. Sullivan, of course, knew that the firing was to be done, but had insisted that Bob wait until he was out of town.

"It was something that built up," Wray, who now lives in North Carolina, says. "It was most unprofessional, coming at the end of a season when it was too late for me to line up something else, and without any apparent motive. Precht and I did not get along at all. He was willful, irresponsible, and given to violent rages."

In retrospect, Precht's motives seem fairly clear. Wray's experience as a director was almost totally studio-oriented. Part of Precht's plan to revitalize the show was to take the show on the road more, to do location programs from different cities around the country. For that, Tim Kiley seemed perfectly suited.

Kiley, then thirty-four, a Northwestern University graduate, had been a staff director at CBS for several years, specializing in the Sunday morning public affairs programs. One of the show's he had done was called *Let's Take a Trip*. Each week, host Sonny Fox would take kids someplace where, it was assumed, kids would like to go. One week it would be an aircraft carrier, another it might be West Point, and still another it might be a visit to a tunnel being dug under the East River. It was complicated stuff, done live, and Kiley had handled it well.

Although Kiley had never done a variety show, Precht knew that he had handled dance and singing on programs like *Camera Three* and *Look Up and Live*. Precht had in the works a program to be done live from Chicago featuring famous Chicagoans like Benny Goodman and Mahalia Jackson. This, he figured, would be a perfect time to test Kiley.

"I was pretty nervous," says Kiley. "This was my first prime time show but I must have done pretty well because shortly after that Bob asked me to come to the Sullivan show.

"To tell you the truth, I wasn't surprised that he was changing directors. It's sort of traditional in this business that a new producer brings in his own people. I guess I never really knew that Sullivan and Wray were close friends."

If, by now, Sullivan suspected that his son-in-law was systematically dismantling the old Sullivan guard and replacing it with troops loyal to himself, he never said so. Kiley remembers him as being extremely gracious when they met.

"Timothy Kiley, uh," Sullivan said. "Well, it's good to see an Irish lad get ahead."

By 1963, Sullivan and his son-in-law had struck a workable truce. Sullivan was in command onstage and Precht ran everything else. Ed was still free to re-routine the show after the dress rehearsal, but he no longer killed acts quite as arbitrarily as he had in the past. Precht did his job quietly, attributed any successes to Sullivan, and took the rap for any mistakes. In return, he was totally free to deal with all details of the mounting of the show, from budgeting to what color to paint the stage floor. He was now completely in charge of the creative staff and, within the scope of union rules, the CBS technical crew.

At this point, the only holdovers from the Marlo Lewis days were Ray Bloch, Bob Arthur, and Jacques Andre. Sullivan was deeply loyal to Bloch, who had been with him from the beginning; Precht liked Arthur both personally and professionally; but Andre, whose title was assistant to the producer, was vulnerable.

During the spring of 1963, Precht came down with pleurisy and was away from the show for a couple of weeks. In his absence, Andre pretty much acted as producer. When Bob returned, Sullivan made it a point to tell him what a terrific job Andre had done in his expanded role.

At the end of the summer, right before Labor Day, Andre was vacationing in Vermont when he got a telegram from Precht asking him to come down for a meeting. Andre thought perhaps Precht wanted to talk to him about a location show or something like that. He was shocked to learn that the reason for the meeting was that he was being fired.

"Bob told me he thought we really shouldn't start the new season together," recalls Andre. "I was very upset and disappointed. The timing was bad, coming as it did at the beginning of the season. I felt I had always been loyal to Bob and that he was a very capable producer.

"The next year, he hired me to work as associate producer on an Al Hirt summer series he was doing. He told me then that he thought he had made a mistake in letting me go. Still, it didn't quite erase the hurt that I felt."

It was during the early Sixties that Sullivan's family realized that he was beginning to get a little senile. It was not until 1966 that hardening of the arteries was diagnosed but his troubles had been building up for a number of years. No doubt it was this problem that led to some of his famous gaffes:

"Good night, and help stamp out TV." (He meant TB.)

Introducing Rich Little: "Let's hear it for this fine young Canadian comic, Buddy Rich."

After Sergio Franchi had finished singing: "C'mon . . . let's hear it for the Lord's Prayer."

Wishing a speedy recovery to Bob Precht, home nursing a cold . . . "Best wishes to our producer, Bob Hope."

"I'd like to *prevent* Robert Merrill."

174

Bob Newhart recalls a time when he was on the show and Sullivan had one of his favorite kind of novelty acts on, two guys who spun plates on top of sticks. "These guys do their bit and Ed, for some reason or another, decides that he wants to talk to them. So he calls them over. Now, these guys are French and neither one of them speaks a word of English. 'Where are you fellows from?' he asks. They just look at each other. Then one of them starts to mumble something in French. 'No, no,' Ed says, 'where are you from?' They're really panicked now and they're jabbering to each other and finally Ed hears the word 'Paris.' 'Paris, um, well, you give my regards to Marshall De Gaulle when you get back.'"

Perhaps the funniest incident was the night he began introducing Dolores Gray in the audience by saying "Now *starving* on Broadway. . . ." This caused him to break himself up and when Gray—who had put on a little weight—took a bow, Sullivan compounded the offense by saying: "Well, you can tell by looking at her that she's not starving."

Not all of Sullivan's forgetfulness was funny, however. Once he had golfer Byron Nelson on the show to give an exhibition of putting. During the number right before Nelson was scheduled, Sullivan signaled a stagehand to get the golf mat ready. He turned his attention elsewhere for a moment and then turned back to see the poor man putting the mat down. He immediately blew his stack and fired the stagehand during the next commercial. No one, even eyewitnesses, could convince him that he had signaled the man to begin.

If the Paar feud showed Sullivan at his darkest, most cantankerous, his relationship with a ten-inch, half-pound foam rubber puppet named Topo Gigo had quite an opposite effect. Of all the devices Sullivan had come up with to display his "humanness" (the hecklers and the mimics), none came close to showing the warm, sympathetic side of Ed as well as the "Little Italian Mouse."

Topo made his debut on April 14, 1963, and was an

immediate sensation. The official word was that Ed had "discovered" Topo when a producer showed him a film of the cuddly little fella in England. Forgotten, apparently, was the fact that talent coordinator Jack Babb had seen Topo first in Italy and had arranged for Ed to see the film.

Unlike most other puppets, Topo was controlled by sticks, not strings. Three expert puppeteers, garbed in black hoods and black velour clothing, manipulated him with their own hands and three-inch sticks. The TV audience couldn't see their intricate, ingenious workings with the mouse as they conducted the entire operations against a black background. The black clothing rendered them practically invisible.

Maria Perego, Topo's creator, was in charge of moving the mouse's feet and controlling the movements of his mouth. Frederico Gioli guided Topo's hands and his wife, Annabella, controlled the puppet's immense ears.

Guiseppe Mazzullo was offstage and it was he who put endearing words into the little mouse's mouth, like the memorable: "Kees-a-me goo' night, Eddie."

The Topo bit always drove the production people crazy. None of the Italians spoke English very well, so proper coordination of the skit depended on Sullivan saying the right thing at the right time. Since he seldom said the same thing twice, this was always scary.

Sullivan professed a genuine affection for his little friend. "When he's on my arm, I actually feel that he's a living thing, and that I'm talking to somebody," he said. "I've never had that feeling before with any puppet or ventriloquist's dummy."

Sullivan always refused to introduce the puppeteers because he didn't want to spoil the Topo illusion.

Over the next few months, Topo made many guest appearances on the show; so many, in fact, that viewers started getting tired of him. He had run into that peculiar show business problem known as overexposure. Gradually, Topo faded back into oblivion, joining Jerry Mahoney and Velvel in dummy heaven.

"I was happy to see Topo go," conceded Jack Babb. "Frankly, I think we wore the little bastard into the ground."

In any event, Sullivan was about to latch onto a set of cuddly lads from Liverpool and they were to create the biggest sensation in the history of the show. They were called the Beatles.

The Beatles

One cold, windy day just before Christmas, 1963, Bob Precht got a call from Sullivan asking him to come over to meet a Mr. Brian Epstein, the manager of a British singing group called the Beatles. Bob had never heard of Epstein, or the Beatles, either, for that matter, but he dutifully dropped what he was doing and headed for the Delmonico.

As he entered Suite 1120, for years the apartment-office-epicenter of Sullivan enterprises, he thought again how strange that a man as famous and well-off as his father-in-law would choose to live and work in a space so small. Only a sedate Renoir painting hanging over the sofa suggested that a man of means lived there. He hung his top coat in a hall closet, bent down to pet the Sullivans' pet poodle Bojangles, and entered the living room where Ed and Epstein were sitting.

"This is Brian Epstein," Sullivan said. "He's got a great group of youngsters. They're going to be real big."

Precht nodded politely. He had met dozens of managers of rock 'n' roll groups that were going to be big.

Epstein turned out to be a polished, round-faced, slightly effeminate man, who was elegantly but conservatively dressed. Precht could tell from the way he and Sullivan were talking that a deal had already been made. This annoyed him. He had asked Ed a number of times not to book acts without telling him.

He almost winced when he realized that the booking was for three shows at $4,000 apiece but he said nothing. A few minutes later, he excused himself and returned to his office where he immediately called Sullivan.

"Ed, Jesus," he said, "Four thousand bucks for some unknown rock 'n' roll group. And three shows?"

It amuses Precht to tell this story nowadays. The Beatles did, indeed, become big and they were to give the Sullivan show the two highest rated programs in its history.

Sullivan had accidentally stumbled into the world of Beatlemania several weeks earlier when passing through the London airport. The prime minister was attempting to fly out to Scotland and the Queen Mother was arriving from Ireland but both were finding travel difficult because of the huge crowd—about 15,000 kids—that had turned out to greet the Beatles, returning from a tour of Sweden. Sullivan didn't care much for rock 'n' roll, but he knew crowds. He was impressed.

Actually, the Beatles were already big international stars by the time Sullivan "found" them, with record sales topping the eleven million mark. "She Loves You" had become the first-ever million selling record in England and the lads from Liverpool by then had more than 400 imitators.

The United States, though, had seemed strangely indifferent to them. "Please, Please Me" was released here in the spring of 1963 and "She Loves You" in the fall. Neither had caused much of a stir.

That's why Brian Epstein had been most pleased to hear of Sullivan's interest and it is also the most likely reason Sullivan was able to get the group so cheaply. The Beatles needed the

United States exposure the Sullivan show could give them.

Epstein and Sullivan agreed on dates—February 9 and 16, with a taped appearance to be played later. Epstein figured that would give him enough time to persuade Capitol Records, the Beatles' United States representative, to mount a massive publicity campaign and to release "I Want to Hold Your Hand," the single that would determine if his group was going to make it in America or not. (Actually a Washington disc jockey named Carroll James had already had a friend—a BOAC stewardess—bring him a copy in early December and as a result of his constant play of the song, D.C. record shops were flooded with requests for a recording that hadn't been released in the United States yet.) This, Epstein knew, was a good sign.

Capitol was willing. Five million "The Beatles Are Coming" stickers were printed and distributed. "Be a Beatles Booster" buttons were readied, along with Beatles wigs. A Capitol representative even tried—unsuccessfully—to bribe a University of Washington cheerleader to have the cheering section hold up "The Beatles Are Coming" cards in the Rose Bowl.

Epstein visited the most influential New York disc jockeys, concentrating on the big rock stations like WMCA and WABC, and promising exclusive interviews and promotions with the lads once they arrived on these shores.

Everything went exactly as planned. "I Want to Hold Your Hand" was released in early January and by the end of the month had reached the number one spot on the record charts. A carefully primed nation waited breathlessly for the arrival of the Beatles.

A combination of circumstances had conspired to make the emergence of the Beatles especially timely. Most of the nation's young people were still in something akin to a state of shock because of the assassination of President Kennedy three months earlier. To some the Beatles represented nothing more than a bit of relief from the despair that had engulfed them. To others, more bitter, the Beatles represented the beginning of a rebellion. To them, the Beatles were to be the Fort Sumter of the War of the Sixties.

In any event, B-Day—the day the Beatles discovered America—was February 7, 1964. By dawn, half of the teen-agers from Morristown, New Jersey, to Stamford, Connecticut, were gathered at the international terminal at Kennedy Airport. They all had transistors plugged into their craniums. It was like a scene from *Invasion of the Body Snatchers*. The radio stations relentlessly fed them Beatles bulletins: "They left London an hour ago. . . . They're on their way."

By one o'clock, there were about 5,000 kids at the airport, watched over by 110 policemen. At 1:20 P.M., the chartered plane arrived. A huge roar went up from the crowd.

It grew into an ear-shattering salute as John, Paul, George, and Ringo descended from the plane, waved, and headed for customs and a prearranged news conference inside. Actually, the Beatles hardly looked like rebels. Epstein had gotten them up in four-button coats, stovepipe pants, ankle-high boots with Cuban heels, and white shirts with ties.

The scene inside at the press conference was no less a madhouse. The New York press corps, never known for its good manners, was outdoing itself with even more than the usual pushing, shoving, shouting, cursing, and occasional punching.

Brian Somerville, the Beatles' press agent, took to the microphone and said "Ladies and Gentlemen, this is ridiculous. Hold up your hands, and I'll recognize you one at a time. If you won't be quiet, we'll just stand here until you are." His stern school teacher manner worked and order, more or less, prevailed. The Beatles were witty and charming and despite the fact that some of the questions were asked by Capitol Records representatives who already knew the answers, they easily won the day.

"What do you think of Beethoven?" someone asked John.

"Lovely writer," Lennon said, "especially the poems."

182

"What are you going to do about the car-bumper stickers in Detroit that say 'Stamp Out the Beatles?'"

"We're printing some that say 'Stamp Out Detroit,'" George replied.

"Are you part of a social rebellion against the older generation?"

"It's a dirty lie," said Paul.

"How do you find America?"

"Go to Greenland and take a left," said Ringo.

"What don't you like about America?"

"Well," George said. "I don't much like your tie."

All in all, it was a tour de force for the working class heroes from Liverpool. After the press conference, they all piled into limousines—one Beatle to each—and headed for the Plaza Hotel.

The Plaza, one of the oldest and most staid of New York hotels, was not exactly thrilled at what was happening. The Beatles had booked rooms a couple of months in advance under their individual names. Management had no idea it had agreed to lodge a social phenomenon. Now there were all these kids, mainly girls, gathered outside, yelling and screaming, and threatening to burst through the police barriers at any moment.

One hotel spokesman told the press that while the Beatles weren't consistent with the Plaza "image," the official position was that they did have reservations, they could pay their bills, they were behaving nicely, and it would be all over in a few days.

Meanwhile, the vigil outside continued. Some clever girls tried having taxi cabs deposit them at the doorstep of the hotel and telling the security men that they had rooms there. It didn't work. Others tried, unsuccessfully, to get onto the rooftops of adjoining buildings. Periodic chants of "We Want Ringo" rose up throughout the night.

The next day, Saturday, the Beatles made two forays over to the Sullivan studio on Broadway and 53rd Street where another

183

crowd had gathered. They ran through their numbers, humming mostly, while Precht and his crew checked camera angles and that sort of thing. George, who had a slight cold, was left behind at the Plaza and their road manager, Neil Aspinall, stood in for him at the rehearsal.

A bulletin was released to the press assuring them that George would be rehabilitated in time for the show. "He'd better be," joked Sullivan, "or I'll put on a wig myself."

At 2:30 the next day, Sunday, all four of the Beatles gathered at the studio for the dress rehearsal and to tape a couple of numbers for a future appearance. The 728-seat capacity theater was filled with teen-age girls, many of them daughters of CBS or Capitol executives. Although he was still sore at Jack Paar, who had slightly scooped him with a taped preview of the Beatles on January 3, Sullivan made it a point to see that Paar's daughter, Randy, got a seat. In all, the show had over 50,000 requests for tickets to the rehearsal and the show itself.

As Sullivan sat backstage writing out some notes for the show, he was approached by Brian Epstein who said, "I would like to know the exact wording of your introduction."

Sullivan, his nerves a little on edge from the strain, didn't even look up from his notepad.

"I would like for you to get lost," he said.

As Ringo's drums were wheeled onstage, a great roar went up from the crowd. A few minutes later, Sullivan appeared. He made a nice speech about how he hoped the kids would give their respectful attention to the other performers on the show because if they didn't, he would call in a barber. The kids laughed in that nervous sort of way that meant that they thought he just might.

After a little more clowning around, Sullivan said, "Our city—indeed, the country—has never seen anything like these four young men from Liverpool. Ladies and gentlemen, the Beatles."

Amidst a tornado of hysteria, the Beatles sang "She Loves You" and "I Want to Hold Your Hand."

In the control room, Bob Precht watched the monitors and mumbled to nobody in particular, "Jesus Christ." It was, he had to admit, the damnedest thing he had ever seen.

The show that night went exactly the same way, except that the hysteria was even more pronounced. Sullivan was delighted, although he figured he would be in for some grief for leading the youth of America astray.

Whatever misgivings he might have had disappeared the next morning when the preliminary ratings indicated that the show might have been of record proportions. He decided then and there to use the taped appearance on February 23. Better to strike while these youngsters were hot, he reasoned.

After the show, the Beatles dropped by the Playboy Club, which is nearby the Plaza, and Paul admitted that the bunnies were "even cuter than us." After that, they went by the Peppermint Lounge, the home of the twist. "It wasn't a bit like us," Ringo said. "The music was too good."

The next morning, the papers filled with analysis of the fab four and their impact on America. Said John Hughes in the *Christian Science Monitor*:

"Britons and Americans may have had their differences over Suez and Skybolt. There was even quite a to-do over the Boston Tea Party. But for sheer British ruthlessness, nothing can compare with the dispatch to the United States of four screaming, strumming, young Liverpudlians with golliwog haircuts known as the Beatles."

Dr. Joyce Brothers wrote in the *Journal-American*:

"The Beatles display a few mannerisms which almost seem a shade on the feminine side, such as the tossing of their long manes of hair. . . . These are exactly the mannerisms which very young female fans (in the 10-to-14 age group) appear to go wildest over."

For sheer humor, though, nothing could match Theodore Strongin's comments in the *Times*:

"The Beatles are directly in the mainstream of Western tradition; that much may be immediately ascertained. Their harmony is unmistakeably diatonic. A learned British colleague, writing on his home ground, has described it as a pandiatonic, but I disagree.

"The Beatles have a tendency to build phrases around unresolved leading tones. This precipitates the ear into a false modal frame that temporarily turns the fifth of the scale into the tonic, momentarily suggesting the Mixylydian mode. But everything always ends as plain diatonic all the same.

"Meanwhile, the result is the addition of a very, very slight touch of British countryside nostalgia, with a trace of Vaughan Williams, to the familiar elements of the rock 'n' roll prototype."

On Wednesday, the Beatles did two sold-out concerts at Carnegie Hall and then on Thursday headed for Miami where the Sullivan show was set to originate from the Deauville Hotel on Sunday. Because of the heavy demand for tickets, the show was shifted from the Casanova Room, to the outdoors area, and finally to the huge Napoleon Room which seated over 3,000 when set up theater-style.

The most anxious moment came about thirty seconds before air time when it became apparent that the Beatles themselves couldn't get into the room because of the crush of people congested around the door. Since they were scheduled to open the show, a wave of panic shot through the Sullivan production people. About fifteen seconds before they were scheduled to appear, a group of Miami policemen formed a flying wedge around the group and stormed the door, sending bodies scattering in all directions. Two seconds after he got to his drums, Ringo found himself being cued to start playing.

It was about this time that the huge crowd outside the hotel noticed the CBS control truck parked outside. Since they couldn't get in, they apparently figured the next best thing would be to watch the show on the monitors inside the truck.

Bill Bohnert was standing behind the console where Tim Kiley and the technical director were working when he glanced

186

up and saw a great wave of humanity rushing toward the truck. He dived over the console, reached the door and bolted it just before the first wave hit. Throughout the show, the men inside feared for their lives and the kids outside rocked the truck up and down. By some miracle, the equipment remained intact and the program stayed on the air.

On Monday, Sullivan got the good news. The weekly Neilsens, the new popularity poll which had replaced Trendex, indicated a score of 44.6 for the first show. That translated to 73,900,000 viewers—the largest audience in television history up to that time. Sullivan was beside himself with joy. It was the first time in seven years that he had topped the ratings.

The Miami telecast was only slightly less successful with a forty-three point two. Today, the two shows rank tenth and seventeenth on the all-time list of most-watched programs. Oddly enough, ratings for the taped appearance on February 23 were only average.

In a sense, the Beatles programs were a last hurrah for Sullivan. Never again would his show attain the prominence that the Beatles had given him, nor would so much attention from an entire nation be focused on his doings. He kept trying, though, and over the next few months, most of the popular British groups—The Dave Clark Five, Gerry and the Pacemakers, The Rolling Stones—appeared on his stage.

The Beatles returned to the United States in August 1964, but this time Epstein wanted a lot of money for a television appearance. Sullivan bowed out of the negotiations early and said he wished them the best. No doubt he was sincere because when no hotel wanted to put them up, he interceded with the management of his own, the Delmonico, to get them lodging.

ABC and CBS both negotiated for taped appearances which they showed during the November "ratings week." Both were ratings disasters. ABC showed its Beatles show taped in London opposite Sullivan and Walt Disney on a Sunday night.

Sullivan and Disney won handily. One of the first people to telephone the news around town was Ed Sullivan.

It was nothing personal, of course, just show business.

As it happened, Sullivan *was* back in the news that fall, but in a way he never quite intended. The reason was a run-in with a young comic named Jackie Mason and it was an ugly scene.

The Comic

Jackie Mason has the appearance of a man who has watched too many dreams go down the drain. At forty-nine, he seems a man without a great deal of optimism, an entertainer whose performing psyche took sick one night in Detroit or Cleveland and never quite recovered. He seems to suffer from too many nights in too many towns; too many audiences that didn't laugh quite enough; too many agents who said "Jackie, baby, have I got a project for you."

"You look like Jackie Mason," our waitress says.

"I ought to," Jackie replies. "I've been paying his bills for forty years." There is no hint of humor in the line, just a statement of fact.

He is wearing a polyester sports jacket, shirt collar open at the top, Gucci shoes with shiny gold buckles. He could be an insurance salesman from Los Angeles up at Vegas for a weekend of craps.

"What are you, a gentile?" he asks. That isn't a joke either, just curiosity.

There was a time, only fifteen or so years ago, when Mason was the brightest young comedy star in the country. With his deadpan face and heavy Jewish accent, he could make people laugh reading a phone book. Forget Lenny Bruce. Mason was much funnier. Gentiles loved his Sam-the-tailor delivery. Ethnic humor was in.

The Sullivan show made Mason a star. He earned the top price of $7,500 an appearance and commanded nightclub fees of around $300,000 a year. Today, both he and the I.R.S. wonder where a lot of it went.

Like most comics, Mason hated doing the Sullivan show. It was, for comedians, a form of slow death. The business of making people laugh is terrifying enough under the best circumstances. Working for Sullivan was the worst. Singers could always hide behind their arrangements, jugglers got a second chance to complete their tricks, but the comics stood alone on the stage. If the audience didn't laugh, they were dead and they knew it.

Sullivan had a mortal fear of words. Even established funnymen had to run through their routines, just as they planned to say it, for him in his office a few days before the show. He never laughed, merely grunted. If he thought something was not funny or slightly off-color, he would say so and it would be cut out of the routine. This run-through was agony for everyone who endured it.

Then came the Sunday dress rehearsal. Sullivan would stand in the wings, watching the audience's reaction. If they laughed, he laughed. If not, the comic's act would be trimmed by a couple of minutes or, worst of all, Bob Precht or Mark Leddy or Jack Babb would be sent to tell the comic's agent that his client's services would not be required.

No other show on the air ever screened comedians' material more carefully or dealt with the performers in such a cavalier manner. Still, most of the comedians put up with it because the Sullivan show was the big shot, the one appearance that could make them a household name, confirmation that they were good and important.

One man who didn't choose to go through the process is now a famous and very successful Las Vegas comic. This comic—let's call him Morty—was on the show once and he deviated from his prepared material to observe that it didn't really take much talent to appear on the show—after all, he said, "Look at Ed." Sullivan was furious. As the performer walked offstage, Sullivan walked up and poked him hard in the chest with his finger and said, "Look, you bastard, I've got more talent in my little finger than you shit comics have in your whole bodies." The comic, a big guy, just laughed and kept walking.

A few days later, Sullivan got a call from someone he thought was the impertinent comic's manager. "Listen, Ed," the voice on the phone said, "the kid is really sorry about what happened. He really needs a break. He won't ever do that kind of thing again."

After about a half hour of pleading, Sullivan relented. "Well, all right," he said, "he can come on again, but he'd better behave himself."

"Ed," the voice said.

"Yeah," Sullivan said.

"Ed," the voice said, "this is Morty. Fuck you. I don't want to be on your show."

Only one other comic ever had that kind of courage with Sullivan and it cost him dearly. His name was Jackie Mason.

It happened the night of October 18, 1964. The show was interrupted halfway through, at 8:30, for an address by President Johnson, but continued in the studio in the expectation that the address might not last a full half-hour. As fate would have it, it didn't. When normal programming resumed, Mason was onstage. He was, he admits, already annoyed at having been scheduled last.

"I was doing my monologue," Mason says, "and he goes like this to me to tell me I got two minutes left. You couldn't see it

191

at home on television but the studio audience was watching him walking around giving me gestures. He was too stupid to do it like most people . . . get behind a camera and hide and give you a gesture. He was making it very obvious to the whole studio audience that he's giving me gestures. So before you know it, my punch lines started bombing. Everybody was watching his fingers. So I decided to make fun of those fingers, so people should understand why I'm not getting laughs. 'They didn't come to watch your fingers. They came to watch my act. You got fingers for them. I got fingers for you. You want a finger, here's a finger. Here's another finger.' Well, I got big, big laughs. I thought I was a sensation. . . . I thought that after the show he'd walk over and thank me for being such a hit because I thought I ad-libbed my way out of a tough situation.

"So, when they told me he wanted to see me after the show, I said 'Great, I'll be right down.' I come downstairs. . . . 'You sonofabitch, . . . I thought at first it was some kind of joke. I thought he was expressing love to me in a strange way. . . .''

Mason surveys the table for reaction to this tale and his eyes light up a bit. The gentile is laughing.

"So when he started to curse I said, 'Wait a minute, let me explain something.' And he said 'What explain, you phoney bastard. I'll wipe you out if it's the last thing I do. You fuckin' sonofabitch. Who the fuck are you to make fingers at me?' I said 'I wasn't. . . .' 'You were, you phony bastard. Fuck you. Drop dead. I'll kill you. I'll wipe you out. I'll make sure you never work in show business again.'

"So, I see that I'm dealing with a crazy person and I walk away from him. To tell you the truth, I really didn't care at that time. His was a tougher show to do than any of the others because of his strong and murderously intimidating personality. It was never a picnic to do his show."

The gravity of the situation came home to Mason not long after, though. Sullivan sent a wire to each of the city's newspapers which said: "Bob Precht, producer of *The Ed*

Sullivan Show, announced that he cancelled Jackie Mason's contract, which calls for six appearances on the program, as a result of Mason's on-camera obscene gestures, offensive conduct, insubordination, and gross deviation from material agreed upon on the telecast tonight."

With five appearances left on the contract, that meant $37,500 to Mason, not a sum to be sneezed at.

"Still," Mason says, "I was getting so much publicity, I figured I had to be the world's biggest star. Guys were calling me from Tokyo. I was getting calls in the middle of the night. 'Hel-ro, this is Tok-yo. He leally say fruck you?'"

Mason figured the whole thing would blow over before long but as the weeks went by and he began having trouble finding club dates, the reality of the situation set in. Sullivan really was planning to freeze him out of the business. Three months after the appearance, Mason filed a libel and slander suit in the New York supreme court charging Sullivan with "maliciously and wickedly contriving to injure, blacken, and defame the plaintiff in his character, reputation, profession, and calling."

Like most suits of that type, it went nowhere fast and Mason continued to struggle to find work. A year or so after the incident, Mason's agent started feeling Sullivan out about the possibility of a reconciliation. At first, Sullivan wasn't having any, but as the months went by, he began to soften.

The popular version of the reconciliation goes like this: Sullivan sees Mason in the Las Vegas airport. He recognizes the face but can't quite place the name. He goes over and throws his arms around Mason and says, "How are you? Why haven't you been on my show lately?" The story has some plausibility because it supposedly happened in the summer of 1966, about the time that arteriosclerosis began to take its toll on Sullivan's memory. Mason tends to nod mysteriously when this version is mentioned. It's too good a story to trifle with.

In any event, on Sunday September 11, 1966, at the end of the show, Sullivan announced that next Sunday, "Highlighting the show will be an old friend of mine and yours, Jackie Mason." Mason then joined Sullivan onstage and everyone shook hands and smiled a lot.

The next Sunday, Mason came on, did his act, got lots of laughs, and was never invited back.

"I'm sure he was a nice man," Mason says. "Offstage he was sweet and generous and pleasant. On the show, he was a tyrant. There are people like that."

The Curtain
1965–1971

The years between 1965 and 1971 were among the most turbulent in American history. The Sullivan show limped on, a kind of living antique, its jugglers and clowns and dancing bears a touching reminder of more peaceful times. Bob Precht, who was very much the major figure during this period, tried to walk the high wire that separated young from old. It was an impossible feat.

The bedrock of the show's support was people in the middle and older age groups but they alone could not carry the show in the ratings. To attract younger viewers meant booking more rock 'n' roll artists, a move that inevitably alienated many of the older regulars. To complicate matters, the networks and advertising agencies had reached the conclusion that it is young people who buy things. Old people generally have already made all the major purchases they're going to make. Thus, a show had to have a significant viewership in the eighteen- to thirty-five-year-old age group to have currency.

If Precht had shown signs of being an innovative producer in the early Sixties, that impulse was now somehow lost amidst the problems of week-to-week survival. The Sullivan show could not compete with real life. It was an anachronism, carried on mainly by force of habit.

Each year CBS would send around a form asking what Sullivan Productions planned to do the next year. Bob took it very seriously, but Sullivan always said, "Fuck 'em. We'll do the same thing we did last year."

A bright spot during those years came on December 10, 1967, when CBS renamed Studio 50 The Ed Sullivan Theatre. He was the first television personality to receive that kind of accolade. Sullivan, then sixty-five and in failing health, was touched. He also felt it was about time the network did something to show its gratitude.

Actually, CBS had some big problems to deal with. Despite its long reign as king of the television hill, the network had developed the reputation of being the "granny" of the majors. Its shows were basically put together by older people for an audience of older people.

Although they continued to book rock groups in an effort to win younger viewers, there were two incidents in the mid-Sixties that soured Precht and Sullivan forever on the subject.

One was a near miss and the other was a real tragedy.

When the Rolling Stones came to the studio to rehearse, a large crowd gathered outside hoping to get a glimpse of the group. Against the advice of Sullivan production people, the members of the group decided to leave the studio to get something to eat. They made it out to their car all right, but when they returned the size of the crowd had tripled. There simply was no way to get back in the stage door. After driving around the block several times, they decided to make a run for the front door of the theater. This seemed a reasonably safe bet because most of the crowd was around the corner at the stage door.

The limousine stopped and Mick Jagger, Keith Richard, and the others scrambled for the door. Unfortunately, it was locked. By now the crowd had gotten the word and had rushed around to the front entrance. Jagger and the Stones' manager were forced right through the plate glass doors. Incredibly, they had only minor cuts, but it had been a close call.

The other, more tragic, incident happened shortly after. A high school student had requested and received a press pass to cover the visit of Herman's Hermits to the Sullivan stage. He had hung around backstage during the program and shortly afterward departed by the stage door.

The boy, good-looking with long hair, found himself surrounded by a mob, all of whom thought he was one of the Hermits. Hands were tearing at his clothes. He felt as though he was being smothered. He fought his way furiously through the mob and dived frantically into the street just in time to be struck by a passing automobile. He was killed instantly.

After that, Sullivan and Precht tried to stay away from groups that might incite a riot or attract large, potentially violent crowds.

Precht did not plan to go down without a good fight, however, and he drove himself and his staff even harder. His production staff, already the hardest working in television, were asked to do even more.

Russ Petranto, then twenty-six, came to the show in 1967 as a production assistant and found himself inundated in work. Petranto, who had come to CBS four years earlier directly from the same New York University film and television class that had produced movie director Martin Scorsese, was a valuable addition to the team. He found the pace exhilarating and exhausting.

"I once spent forty-eight hours straight editing a tape for the show," he recalls. "I finished at about six in the morning on Sunday and took it to Bob and told him I had to go home and shower and put on some clean clothes. I suppose I slept for about an hour. When I got back to the studio at about noon, Bob told me he wanted the whole piece re-done. Bob Arthur and I went back to the control room, and somehow we finished it in time for the show. I could have killed Bob at the time, but—in retrospect—it was marvelous training."

Despite the Herculean efforts, however, the handwriting was clearly on the wall for the Sullivan show. The number of variety shows on the air had swelled to more than twenty by 1969. There was no such thing as fresh talent any more. Clearly something had to give.

Tim Kiley was one of the first to recognize that the end was near and shortly after Christmas 1969, he left for California.

Bob Schwarz, who had been assistant director for only about three months, couldn't quite believe it when Precht approached him on a Thursday and said he could direct the show on Sunday if he wanted to. As it turned out, his good fortune was just a little too good to last.

"Johnny Moffet had been assistant director for a long time," Schwarz recalls, "and he had left before I came because there didn't seem to be any place for him to go. He was out in Hawaii directing a Glenn Yarborough special. Johnny is one of those forceful little characters who always knew what they wanted to do. I can just imagine him on the phone to Precht: 'Christ, Bob, I've been working on the show for nine years and this guy's been there three months.' In any event, John came back and we shared the director's responsibility. He did about three-fifths of the shows and I did the other two-fifths.

"It was very decent of Bob to keep us both on and, actually, pretty smart, too. I think he didn't want to be left without a director the way he was when Tim left. My relationship to Precht was pretty much boss-employee, but I owe him and I think he built a tremendous production team. It always sort of amazed me that we could go into a town on a Thursday and have a very decent show on the air by Sunday."

The last point is an interesting one because it comes directly to the heart of whether or not Precht was simply a lucky son-in-law (as some old-timers suggest) or a skilled producer. Unlike a star who is judged by his performance on the air, a producer can only be judged by how smoothly the product he

198

controls operates. This, in turn, is a direct reflection of the skill of people he chooses to employ. A bad producer hires bad people; a good producer surrounds himself with the best talent available.

Judging from the track record of the graduates of Precht's production team, Precht has to be judged a very good producer. Without exception his team members are still employed in important positions in the television industry today.

Consider, for example, the case of Vince Calandra, whose career may be the most dramatic but is by no means untypical.

Today Calandra is the producer of *The Mike Douglas Show*. He began his television career in 1960 as a cue card boy for the Sullivan show.

"I was twenty-six at the time, fresh out of the Army and unemployed," Calandra says. "My aunt met a woman on a cruise to Bermuda and she recommended me to somebody at CBS. My God, it looked hopeless. There were guys in the mail room with degrees from Brown University and here I was going to night school at St. John's."

Calandra, who probably would have been a professional baseball player had he not hurt his arm, approached Marlo Lewis several times about getting something on the Sullivan staff and had no success. When Bob Precht took over, he remembered the nice Italian kid from the mail room and hired Vince to do cue cards.

"I had just gotten married and we were living in this seventy-five-dollar-a-month, two-room place in Brooklyn," Calandra recalls. "My wife would read me lyrics while I copied them onto cards. I remember once doing thirty-five cards for one Alan King monologue."

Calandra has one of those instantly likable personalities and he was quickly adopted by some of the more knowledgeable people on the staff like talent coordinator Jack Babb. Although he never got around to finishing at St. John's, Vince advanced quickly in the organization. He was promoted to production assistant and then when Jack Babb left, he became talent

199

coordinator. It was a job to which he was perfectly suited by temperament and it filled a gap in Precht's personality. Bob himself never really liked show business people very much.

"I took a lot of ribbing around the office after each of my promotions," Calandra says. "We had moved into a house out on Long Island and I remember Bob would come by and say 'Well, you can order your new drapes now,' or somebody else would say, 'Hey, Vinnie. Did you get flamingoes for your lawn yet?'"

It was a great time for Calandra and he got to know everybody who was important in show business, as well as several people who would later achieve a certain kind of prominence.

"I remember a nice English lady who was an assistant to our costume designer, Leslie Renfield. She used to tease me a lot. It was Kay Summersby, who had been Eisenhower's driver during the war," he says. "And there was Michael Bennett, who later did A *Chorus Line*. He was what we called a gypsy. We would hire him to choreograph a show for a flat thousand bucks.

"The funniest one of those I guess was this tall blond kid who used to sneak into our rehearsal hall. Every week I'd go down and find him there and throw him out before Bob arrived. It was Barry Manilow. We had him on *The Mike Douglas Show* last year. When he came in, I said, 'Hi, Barry. Remember me? I used to throw you out of the CBS rehearsal hall.' It cracked him up."

After the Sullivan show folded, Calandra worked for a few months for Paramount Records and then joined the Douglas show staff in Philadelphia as talent coordinator. When Douglas moved to Hollywood this year, Calandra went along as producer.

"If you had told me twenty years ago that I would someday be producer of a major TV show, living in Woodland Hills and driving a Lincoln, I would have said you were crazy," Calandra says. "I owe it all to the Sullivan organization."

The last statement is one you hear frequently from former

members of the Sullivan production staff. There has probably never been a closer knit television organization. The pace of the show and the backbreaking schedule pretty much precluded the kind of petty jealousies and rivalries that usually spring up. After the show on Sunday night, most of the staff would gather next door at a restaurant called the China Song just to unwind.

It is little wonder then that the atmosphere was so emotionally charged during the early months of 1971. A beautifully functioning machine was about to be taken apart.

Perhaps better than anyone, Precht knew what was happening but he simply did not want to let go. Over the last couple of seasons, he launched a series of massive production shows. In several instances—such as a tribute to Richard Rodgers from the Hollywood Bowl—the shows were among the finest ever done by a variety series.

Although they were part of a weekly series (cut back to twenty-four new shows at the beginning of the 1971 season which was, in fact, the standard at the time), Precht attacked several of the key programs as if they were specials. In one period, set designer Bill Bohnert was flying to Toronto with plans for a Muppets Christmas Special, then on to California for the Richard Rodgers show, back to Las Vegas where another show was scheduled, and then back to St. Louis where sets were being built for a program to originate in Atlanta.

"We were spending $50,000 to $60,000 for scenery for a given show, which is a respectable amount for a special even now," says Bohnert. "Our normal budget was around $10,000 to $12,000 per show.

"Toward the end I tried to economize by deliberately building sets that could be re-used later in the season. At one time, we had a warehouse filled with props for the Sullivan show a city block long."

The extra travel involved in the specials was wearing on Sullivan, but he was holding up remarkably well.

One of the specials was an ice show from Las Vegas. A small stage was created by laying a wooden floor over a section of the ice. Sullivan spent nearly twelve hours during rehearsals and the actual show standing on this freezing platform while around him the younger men shivered and turned numb. Somehow, he never seemed to notice.

The shows were terrific but the ratings never really picked up.

"We all read the newspapers," says Tony Jordan, then, as now, production manager of Sullivan Productions. "I guess we all hoped that CBS would give us a couple of more years to make twenty-five."

By the spring of 1971, however, the atmosphere at CBS had reached crisis proportions. For the first time, NBC had edged ahead in the ratings race for an entire season. Obviously, heads were going to roll.

Precht expected the worst and tried to prepare his father-in-law for the bad news. Sullivan was reluctant to believe it could happen. Meanwhile, Precht quietly put out feelers to the other networks. There were no takers.

In March, Sullivan had dropped to forty-third in the ratings with a nineteen share or about twenty-three million viewers. When CBS announced that it was dropping Red Skelton and Jackie Gleason, Precht knew the show was doomed.

Precht had tried every trick he knew. The first half of the year he had tied each program to a theme—an ice show, a visit to a state fair, a salute to the United Nations, the tribute to Richard Rodgers. It had helped some, but not enough.

The call came on March 17. Precht was in the screening room of Sullivan Productions on West 57th Street with Tony Jordan, Vince Calandra, and budget director Bob Spitzer when he was called out to take a phone call in his office.

"I had a sinking feeling as I walked to the phone," Precht says. "I knew this was it."

The caller was CBS president Bob Wood, who had been making bold moves to give the network a more "relevant, now" image. The network strategists had been struggling with the

Sullivan decision for days, weighing its declining viewership against what Wood called its "grand tradition."

Wood said: "We're awfully sorry, Bob, but in view of all the many considerations for the new season, we're going to have to drop the old format. But we don't want to lose the Sullivan production team, and you have a commitment to do six to ten specials."

Precht thanked Wood and returned to the screening room, where he told the others, "The show as we've known it is no more."

For about fifteen of the show's 200 production people (the skeleton staff who belonged to Sullivan Productions rather than CBS), it meant unemployment.

Precht phoned Sullivan at the Delmonico. "Well I'll be a son of a bitch," Sullivan said. "After all we've done for the network over the years."

Sullivan had to content himself with the commitment to specials, but he was very hurt by the cancellation. It wasn't much consolation, but he had to view the CBS move as part of a general housecleaning. With Sullivan, the network also dropped such perennials as *Lassie, Hogan's Heroes, Andy Griffith, Green Acres,* and the most popular comedy series of all time, *The Beverly Hillbillies.*

A few days after the cancellation, Bill Bohnert watched sadly as garbage trucks hauled the props he had been hoarding off to a dump in New Jersey to be burned.

Sullivan didn't have the heart for an emotional farewell, so the last program aired was a repeat featuring Carol Channing, Robert Klein, Caterina Valente, Jerry Vale, Pat Henry, Peter Nero, and Gladys Knight. There was a brief nostalgic moment when Topo Gigo made a return appearance for a final "Kiss-a-me goo' night, Eddie." Then it was gone.

"Rock 'n' roll and reruns, that's what killed the Sullivan

203

show," Mark Leddy says. He is wrong about that. It was the times.

Sullivan's first special in 1972, *The Sullivan Years*, got a whopping forty-three and was the eighth best-rated special of the entire season.

In 1973, he did the second annual "Entertainer of the Year Awards" from Caesar's Palace in Las Vegas on January 15 and racked up an astounding forty-seven, wiping out the opposition, and ending up second only to *All in the Family* in the weekly Neilsens. His second on February 20, a Tuesday night, opposite the incredibly popular *Marcus Welby,* got a forty, and ended up fifth for the week.

His third special of the year, on March 16, called *Ed Sullivan's Broadway* was a winner in the ratings, too, but it really didn't matter. Sylvia, his companion of forty-three years, died the day of the telecast.

Her death, from a ruptured aorta, was a real surprise because she had entered the hospital ostensibly for a checkup.

"It was the biggest shock of my life," says Betty Precht, "because it was so unexpected. Mother looked so young and healthy and was so strong right to the end."

Sylvia and Ed had been particularly close since the cancellation of the show and had traveled widely together. She seemed in near perfect health and looked much younger than her sixty-nine years. Among those who were surprised to learn her real age was her daughter, Betty, who had never really known.

Her only real health problem had come as a result of a minor accident when she was struck by a slow moving car in front of the Alamo in San Antonio the year before. Her Alamo accident had become a kind of family joke, although, in fact, her knee injury had been quite painful. The only person she would allow to touch her and help her walk during her recovery was Carmine Santullo, of Ed's loyal Man-Friday. He had, she said, a delicate touch.

She had ordered a color television set for her room at Mt. Sinai Hospital so she could watch the special.

Sylvia's death was to plunge Sullivan into a deep depression from which he never really emerged. Sylvia was gone, Bob and Betty and the five grandchildren were in Scarsdale. There was no show to look forward to each week. *Ed Sullivan's Broadway* was to be his last show. He spent more time with his sister, Helen, and, particularly, with his friend Carmine.

The Friend

The road is long and filled with many a winding turn. Enemies are everywhere. All men of power need a trusted servant, someone who is absolutely devoted and will do their bidding without many questions, who will remember the good things and forget the bad, someone who owes not only his livelihood but also his station in life to his proximity to that power. Someone, indeed, who loves his master.

Sullivan's trusted servant was Carmine Santullo. They met in 1934 when Sullivan was hosting the *Dawn Patrol Revue* at Loew's State Theatre and Carmine was a sixteen-year-old backstage bootblack. Sullivan would give him a little money to run his column over to the *Daily News* building.

For Carmine, a cobbler's son from the Bronx with five brothers, two sisters, little formal education, and few prospects, it was the beginning of a great, lifelong adventure. He went to work full-time for Sullivan around 1940 as a kind of secretary, assistant, and general factotum. He gathered information for the column, ran errands, made phone calls, arranged things.

Sullivan called him "Carmen." Carmine called Ed "Mr. Sullivan."

Thousands of people in show business came to know Carmine well from the telephone, but most have never met him face-to-face. In his entire career with Sullivan, he was at the studio no more than ten times.

It was Carmine, the former bootblack, who watched Sullivan draw his last breath at Lenox Hill Hospital on October 13, 1974.

"It's strange your coming here today," Carmine said in his office at Sullivan Productions where he then worked. "Today would have been his seventy-sixth birthday—September 28. He and I were born on the same street—114th Street, you know. I was born between First and Pleasant, he was born between Second and Third."

There is a kind of eloquence about Santullo. Thin and wiry, he doesn't look his sixty-one years. He carries himself with an awareness that his special relationship with Sullivan—a man of great power—has vested him with certain responsibilities. He wants to be helpful. He wants to get the facts right.

He lives with his sister in the Bronx. He never married. The Sullivans were his family. On his desk are small pictures of Ed and Sylvia in one of those folding gold leaf frames that you get at a dime store.

When he wants to agree with you he says, in flawless Bronxese: "Definitely . . . a hunnerd percent."

He worked closely with Sullivan, at his apartment; indeed, Carmine was better acquainted with Sullivan's Irish temper than anyone except, perhaps, Sylvia.

Once Sullivan took him along on a trip to California, which was a rare treat because Carmine seldom went anywhere. They arrived at the Beverly Hills Hotel. When the desk clerk presented Sullivan with a check-in form, he simply signed his name. The desk clerk requested additional information, such as address. Sullivan became annoyed. He simply refused to be bothered. Carmine, standing off to one side, offered up the requested information. Once out of earshot, Sullivan whispered in his Man Friday's ear, "You don't watch out, you'll be on the next plane home."

"He had a temper, of course, and naturally I had many experiences with it, but he would soon quiet down," Carmine says. "I always took it that tomorrow is another day and you couldn't let what happened yesterday carry over."

Amazingly, some of Sullivan's closest friends never saw him angry. Bob Weitman, now a TV and movie producer, first met Sullivan in the 1930s when he—Weitman—was managing the Paramount Theater and Ed was doing variety shows.

"He was really a big softy at heart," Weitman recalls. "I remember once he and Sylvia went to Israel with *my* wife Sylvia and me. Ed was very moved by what he saw there. We were in Churchill Hall in Haifa and this ten-year-old kid on crutches—Itzhak Perlman—played the violin. Ed was very touched and he said to me immediately, 'I've got to have that kid on my show.'

"Another time, a few months after we came back, I invited him to go with me to a fund-raising dinner where Abba Eban was the principal speaker. Eban was a wonderful speaker and he finished to thunderous applause. The host whispered to me to ask Ed if he wanted to say a few words. I asked him and he looked shocked: 'I can't follow Eban,' he said. But he did it and he got up and started talking about what he had seen in Israel and his impressions. It was very emotional and I could see the tears welling up in his eyes. Well, he finished and there wasn't a dry eye in the place. He got as big a hand as Eban and people started buying bonds all over again. He was like that."

Carmine loved to arrange surprises for the boss. On a number of occasions he arranged for special guest stars to show up to mark an anniversary show or Ed's birthday. Once he persuaded twenty-two governors to proclaim "Ed Sullivan Day." There are those who say that Carmine really wrote Sullivan's column after Ed lost interest in it around 1960. He denies this is so.

"I may have put together the notes and the items and talked to people on the phone," he says. "But Ed always looked at it and usually changed things. He really wrote it."

The last thing Sylvia Sullivan said to Carmine before she went into the hospital to die was, "Take care of Mr. Sullivan."

Sullivan and Carmine were particularly close after Sylvia died. Ed no longer had the show, nor his wife, and he was in failing health.

He never knew he had had cancer, though. He had been very sick in May of 1974 and was released from the hospital toward the end of the month. He was supposed to see his doctor daily but began going every second day and, finally, once a week. On one of these visits, on September 6, the doctor did additional X-rays. By the time Sullivan had walked the six blocks to the Delmonico Hotel, his doctor had called Bob Precht.

Cancer of the esophagus. Inoperable. The president of the Damon Runyon-Walter Winchell Cancer Fund was dying of cancer.

Sullivan entered Lenox Hill Hospital that day.

Carmine visited every morning and would return after work and stay until 10:30 or 11 o'clock. Bob and Betty had told him that Sullivan's condition was hopeless, but he did his best to remain cheerful. He brought mail and items for the column.

"When are we going home?" Sullivan would ask.

"Maybe tomorrow," Carmine would answer.

Whenever Carmine would leave the room momentarily, Sullivan would always ask him where he had been.

On September 28, his seventy-third birthday, there were two parties, one given by the nurses, and another by close friends who knew it would be his last.

210

At about 3 o'clock on October 13, Sullivan's condition took a turn for the worse. The Prechts rushed to the hospital. They left at 7:30 when Carmine came in. Sullivan was unconscious and breathing heavily.

"I was sitting at his bedside always looking at him to see how he's doing," Carmine says. This conversation is clearly difficult for him, but his face has no expression. He learned his stone-face from the master. "I'm sure he knew I was there."

At 10:30 P.M., Sullivan simply stopped breathing.

It was a Sunday night. Ironically, ABC was telecasting a Frank Sinatra concert "live" that very night from Madison Square Garden. Television was resuscitating a concept that Sullivan had pioneered.

Sullivan left the bulk of his estate, estimated for probate purposes at $450,000, to his daughter, Betty. Certainly, with deferred payments from CBS, the sum was much greater. He left $10,000 to Carmine, more than to any of his brothers or sisters. He left nothing to charity, the will said, because he had done so much during his lifetime.

Santullo's proudest possession, though, is a 1959 Lincoln Continental that Sullivan gave him in 1960. Carmine used the car once in awhile to take the Sullivans' poodle Bojangles home with him when they were out of town. When Sullivan got a new one, he gave the car to Carmine.

"I still have it in my garage," he says. "It's so expensive to operate that I haven't used it, but it's there when I want to use it."

Some three thousand people—celebrities and just plain folks—turned out for Sullivan's funeral at St. Patrick's Cathedral on October 16. It was a cold and rainy day. Cardinal Cooke, who had been ill, insisted upon presiding over the Mass himself.

The hearse rolled up to the cathedral, and eight pallbearers lifted the casket to their shoulders and carried it up the steps to the entrance where it was received by Cardinal Cooke.

Moments later, the eight dark-suited men bore the casket down the center aisle of the cathedral, while mourners jammed the pews.

The casket, placed directly before the altar, was adorned by a white coverlet bearing the two Greek letters *alpha* and *omega,* symbolizing the beginning and the end.

Following the hymn "For All the Saints," sung by the congregation, Msgr. James A. Rigney initiated a Mass of the Resurrection.

"We have been brought here by that strange combination of sorrow and hope," Msgr. Rigney began, alluding to the sorrow of death and the hope of knowing "we are returning our loved one to a Father who loves him more than any of us ever could."

He remarked that for those who knew Sullivan well no eulogy was necessary, while for anybody who may never have known him, a eulogy would be little more than an introduction. So, instead, he read a letter to Sullivan from Cardinal Cooke in which the prelate praised the long-time columnist's "loyalty to truth and his generosity."

Then, Betty Precht and her children left their pew to the right of the casket and carried the wine and bread to the altar for the consecration of the Host.

Mrs. Precht was among the family mourners who included three of Sullivan's sisters and a brother. They sat across the aisle from Mayor Abe Beame, who recalled Sullivan as "a friend who gave so much to New York City and to the world."

Former Mayor John Lindsay described Sullivan as "a great reporter and a special man who was one of the city's treasures."

Others at the Mass included James A. Farley, Van Cliburn, who commended Sullivan for the latter's "faithfulness to the serious arts," Rise Stevens, Ray Bloch, CBS chairman William Paley, and Attorney General Louis Lefkowitz.

Of all the tributes paid to Sullivan, though, none was more eloquent than that of his friend Carmine Santullo. Standing

212

outside the Cathedral, shivering from the cold and his private grief, Carmine looked at the sky that hung like a shroud, as cold and black as a Broadway press agent's heart. "When it rains at a man's funeral," he said, to nobody in particular, "it's just all those angels shedding tears."

Index

221

223

229